SCOTTISH ISLAND KNITS

ROWAN

SCOTTISH ISLAND KNITS

DESIGNS BY **KAFFE FASSETT, DI GILPIN,
SARAH DALLAS, SASHA KAGAN, JEAN MOSS,
BRANDON MABLY, SARAH HATTON**

PHOTOGRAPHED BY **JACQUI HURST**

SCOTTISH ISLAND KNITS

DESIGNS BY **KAFFE FASSETT, DI GILPIN, SARAH DALLAS,
SASHA KAGAN, JEAN MOSS, BRANDON MABLY, SARAH HATTON**

PHOTOGRAPHED BY **JACQUI HURST**

FIRST PUBLISHING IN 2005 BY
**ROWAN YARNS
GREEN LANE MILL
HOLMFIRTH
WEST YORKSHIRE
HD9 2DX**

DESIGNED AND ART DIRECTED BY **GEORGINA RHODES**
AND **RICHARD PROCTOR**
EDITED BY **SALLY HARDING**
STYLED BY **GEORGINA RHODES** AND **SUSAN BERRY**
PATTERN CHECKER **STELLA SMITH**

BRITISH LIBRARY CATALOGUING IN PUBLICATION DATA
A CATALOGUE RECORD OF THIS BOOK IS AVAILABLE FROM
THE BRITISH LIBRARY

ISBN 1-904485-50-2

REPRODUCED BY THE DOT FACTORY IN GREAT BRITAIN
PRINTED BY ORACLE IN GREAT BRITAIN

CONTENTS

INTRODUCTION

The soft texture and beautifully blended colours of our Scottish Tweed pure wool yarns are a great joy for anyone who loves to knit. Rowan have selected the colour palette for the yarns, and the designs created with them, using the islands of the Outer Hebrides as their inspiration.

The mere mention of the islands of the Outer Hebrides conjures up images of a rugged yet desolate landscape, and a remote island community. The islands have long been associated with both weaving and hand-knitting, and the skills of the crofters involved in spinning, weaving and/or knitting the wool of their own black-faced sheep widely acclaimed. The life of the crofter has always been hard, but it has a romantic appeal too, in touch as it is with the simpler life, where nature and its seasons and colours dictate the pace and mood.

Rowan's yarns draw on this heritage and Rowan adds some expertise of their own to produce a blend of pure woollen fibres that is soft but firm, holding its form while offering superb texture and exquisitely subtle colours.

One of the many advantages of this yarn is that it has been developed to have the same tension as Rowan's Yorkshire Tweed across the 4ply, DK, Aran and Chunky weights, so that it would be compatible with many of the existing patterns. Many of you may now want to reach for your old Rowan magazines with the new Scottish Tweed shade card!

The picture on page 99 shows the range of 24 colours that are available in the different yarn weights.

A group of our foremost designers has worked their magic with the yarns to offer a wonderfully diverse collection of sweaters, cardigans, jackets, waistcoats and boleros, plus a blanket and a bag.

We hope that you enjoy making these designs and working with these very special yarns as much as we have enjoyed developing them, and that you find the very different designs in this book both inspirational and practical.

ABOUT THE DESIGNS

The following is a brief outline of the contributions by the different designers:

Kaffe Fassett has designed Daphne in two versions: a cardigan (see pages 12-13) and a sweater (see page 34). Based on a flower motif which covers the body of the sweater and the cardigan, the sleeves are worked in stripes, picked out in the same colours. Kaffe has also designed Backgammon in two versions – a sweater and a slipover (see pages 36-7). The elongated lozenge shapes in subtly different colours echo the markings on a backgammon board, hence the name.

Di Gilpin has created a truly fantastic Mondrian-style blanket, which resembles Joseph's coat of many colours with its brilliant assymetric colour piecing (see pages 24-5). She has also created a great textural cropped top, Maya, worked in one piece from cuff to cuff, which is laced with leather thonging down the sides (see page 19). A similarly textural collar or snood accompanies it (see page 18).

Jean Moss offers two great boleros, Sassy and Tempo, one in soft cream with a lacy diamond pattern on the fronts and sleeves (see page 31) and the other in a rich burgundy with a neat collar (see page 27). She has also designed a stunning cardigan, Sugarbabe, with a Fair Isle yoke and sleeves (see page 14).

Sasha Kagan adds three distinctive pieces to the collection, including a big, bold jacket featuring Scottie dog designs (see pages 20-21) and a funky Hot Stripe Top in a batwing shape (see pages 28-9) plus a ruffled crochet jacket and skirt (pages 17 and 26).

Sarah Dallas has created a wonderful long wrap jacket, Beth, which can be dressed up for nights out or worn casually for a walk on the beach (see page 22).

Brandon Mably has picked up the seascape theme from the islands for Ripple, a sweater for men or women in soft mauves, sage greens and blues reminiscent of a hazy day on the beach in Lewis (see pages 32-3).

Sarah Hatton turns Fair Isle style contemporary with a vivid mauve shoulder bag (see page 35).

DAPHNE CARDIGAN

This sizzling design by Kaffe Fassett, with its big bold flowers and its striped sleeves in matching colours, is really versatile, translating effortlessly from country to town. Wear it dressed down with jeans or a summer skirt, or out on the town with a long black skirt. Pattern on page 47.

SUGARBABE CARDIGAN

As the name implies, this is a really sweet design by Jean Moss, with its pretty Fair Isle yoke in soft mauves, gold and blues, and matching Fair Isle cuffs. The rest of the cardigan has a great textural stitch pattern on the sleeves, lower body, button band and collar. Pattern on page 78.

FRILLY JACKET

This ruffle-edged bolero-style jacket, worked in crochet, matches the ruffle-edged crochet skirt on page 26 (where it is knitted up in a different colourway). The soft blue ruffle around the neck, fronts and cuffs on the jacket picks up the blue in the marled yarn used for the body and sleeves. Pattern on page 91.

MAYA BATWING TOP AND SNOOD

This unusual cropped top, with its heavily textured diamond pattern, is knitted in one piece widthwise. The sleeve cuffs and seams, and the hem, are trimmed with cute little bobbles. The top laces up the sides and along the sleeves seams with leather thonging. It comes with a matching snood or independent collar. Designed by Di Gilpin. Pattern on page 60.

SCOTTIE DOG JACKET

Little Scotties and Westies dance over this jacket designed by Sasha Kagan. The Scotties are picked out in dark grey on mauve and the Westies in white on grey. The long-length jacket with its duffle-type fastening also has a big cosy hood for cold days. Pattern on page 74.

BETH JACKET

A really great jacket by Sarah Dallas.
It wraps around generously in an easy-
fitting style, with a big soft collar and
dropped shoulders. Comfortable and
really easy to wear, it looks great for both
town and country. Pattern on page 40.

MONDRIAN-STYLE BLANKET

With its fantastic range of coloured shapes, resembling a piece of abstract art, this stocking stitch blanket by Di Gilpin is knitted in Scottish Tweed 4ply, DK and Aran, making a wonderful big warm throw. It is lined with Kaffe Fassett's striped Ikat fabric, also by Rowan, which picks up the colours beautifully. Pattern on page 82.

FRILLY SKIRT

The ruffle-trimmed skirt (far left) by Sasha Kagan looks great with the Tempo Bolero by Jean Moss, shown left, or with its own matching jacket (shown on page 17). The waist is finished with a bobble-trimmed cord. Pattern on page 91.

TEMPO BOLERO

This cropped bolero-style cardigan by Jean Moss is an elegant classic. Easy to knit, it would make a great introduction to Scottish Tweed for a first-time knitter. Pattern on page 88.

HOT STRIPE TOP

This sizzling cropped sweater by
Sasha Kagan is knitted with the body and
sleeves in one piece in a fantastic stripe
pattern with varying widths to the stripe,
making glorious use of the range of
colours in Rowan's Scottish Tweed.
Pattern on page 50.

SASSY BOLERO

This crisp little bolero by Jean Moss, with its lacy diamond pattern on the front and sleeves, looks good with pretty much everything. Classic and elegant, it has a youthful appeal that won't go out of fashion. Pattern on page 70.

RIPPLE SWEATER

Echoing the colours of the shoreline on the Outer Hebrides, this classic sweater by Brandon Mably with its soft waves of colour, will appeal to both men and women. The striped standaway ribbed collar and cuffs give it a warm, neat finish. Pattern on page 66.

DAPHNE SWEATER

Here is the sweater version of the
Kaffe Fassett cardigan shown on page
12. Knitted this time in deep green with
a strongly contrasting mauve for the
flowers, this sweater has striped sleeves
in the same colourways as the flowers.
The round neck is flatteringly low cut.
Pattern on page 44.

NESSIE BAG

Fair Isle goes contemporary in this big
shoulder bag by Sarah Hatton with its
colourwork flap and matching little
flowers. The side gussets and strap are
knitted in one piece. Pattern on page 64.

BACKGAMMON

In two versions – a polo-neck sweater and a slipover – this design by Kaffe Fassett is a classic. It makes really wonderful use of the colour range, and is great fun to knit. Patterns on page 54.

PATTERN INSTRUCTIONS

The following knits are all worked with Rowan Scottish Tweed. Please note that in some designs the yarn is used double. Remember to check your tension before starting. Abbreviations used in the patterns, together with information on knitting techniques, are given in the section on Useful Information on pages 96-100.

BETH JACKET
Sarah Dallas

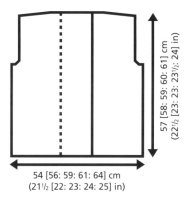

57 [58: 59: 60: 61] cm
(22½ [23: 23: 23½: 24] in)

54 [56: 59: 61: 64] cm
(21½ [22: 23: 24: 25] in)

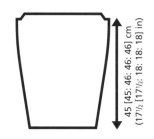

45 [45: 46: 46: 46] cm
(17½ [17½: 18: 18: 18] in)

SIZES & YARNS

XS	S	M	L	XL	

To fit bust

81	86	91	97	102	cm
32	34	36	38	40	in

Rowan Scottish Tweed DK
A Storm grey 004

10	10	11	11	12	x 50gm

B Lewis grey 007

3	3	4	4	4	x 50gm

C Midnight   023

1	1	1	1	1	x 50gm

NEEDLES

1 pair 3¾mm (no 9) (US 5) needles
1 pair 4mm (no 8) (US 6) needles
4.00mm (no 8) (US G6) crochet hook

TENSION

20 sts and 28 rows to 10 cm measured over
stocking stitch, 20 sts and 32 rows to 10 cm
measured over moss stitch, both using 4mm
(US 6) needles.

CROCHET ABBREVIATIONS

ch = chain; ss = slip stitch; dc = double crochet (= US single crochet).

BACK

Using 3¾mm (US 5) needles and yarn B, cast on 107 [111: 117: 121: 127] sts.

Change to 4mm (US 6) needles and beg moss st patt as folls:

Row 1 (RS): K1, *P1, K1, rep from * to end.

Row 2: As row 1.

These 2 rows form moss st.

Cont in moss st until back meas 18 cm, inc 1 st at end of last row and ending with RS facing for next row. 108 [112: 118: 122: 128] sts.

Break off yarn B and join in yarn C.

Beg with a K row, work in st st for 2 rows, ending with RS facing for next row.

Break off yarn C and join in yarn A.

Beg with a K row, cont in st st until back meas 37 [38: 38: 39: 39] cm, ending with RS facing for next row.

Shape armholes

Cast off 4 sts at beg of next 2 rows. 100 [104: 110: 114: 120] sts.

Dec 1 st at each end of next 5 rows. 90 [94: 100: 104: 110] sts.

Cont straight until armhole meas 20 [20: 21: 21: 22] cm, ending with RS facing for next row.

Shape shoulders and back neck

Cast off 8 [8: 9: 9: 10] sts at beg of next 2 rows. 74 [78: 82: 86: 90] sts.

Next row (RS): Cast off 8 [8: 9: 9: 10] sts, K until there are 11 [12: 13: 14: 15] sts on right needle and turn, leaving rem sts on a holder.

Work each side of neck separately.

Cast off 4 sts at beg of next row.

Cast off rem 7 [8: 9: 10: 11] sts.

With RS facing, rejoin yarn to rem sts, cast off centre 36 [38: 38: 40: 40] sts, K to end.

Complete to match first side, reversing shapings.

LEFT FRONT

Using 3¾mm (US 5) needles and yarn B, cast on 67 [69: 71: 73: 77] sts.

Change to 4mm (US 6) needles.

Work in moss st as given for back for 18 cm, inc 0 [0: 1: 1: 0] st at end of last row and ending with RS facing for next row. 67 [69: 72: 74: 77] sts.

Break off yarn B and join in yarn C.

Beg with a K row, work in st st for 2 rows, ending with RS facing for next row.

Break off yarn C and join in yarn A.

Beg with a K row, cont in st st until left front matches back to beg of armhole shaping, ending with RS facing for next row.

Shape armhole

Cast off 4 sts at beg of next row. 63 [65: 68: 70: 73] sts.

Work 1 row.

Dec 1 st at armhole edge of next 5 rows. 58 [60: 63: 65: 68] sts.

Cont straight until left front matches back to beg of shoulder shaping, ending with RS facing for next row.

Shape shoulder

Cast off 8 [8: 9: 9: 10] sts at beg of next and foll alt row, then 7 [8: 9: 10: 11] sts at beg of foll alt row.

Work 1 row, ending with RS facing for next row.

Break yarn and leave rem 35 [36: 36: 37: 37] sts on a holder.

RIGHT FRONT

Using 3¾mm (US 5) needles and yarn B, cast on 67 [69: 71: 73: 77] sts.

Change to 4mm (US 6) needles.

Work in moss st as given for back for 18 cm, inc 0 [0: 1: 1: 0] st at beg of last row and ending with RS facing for next row. 67 [69: 72: 74: 77] sts.

Break off yarn B and join in yarn C.

Beg with a K row, work in st st for 2 rows, ending with RS facing for next row.

Break off yarn C and join in yarn A.

Beg with a K row, cont in st st until right front matches back to beg of armhole shaping, ending with WS facing for next row.

Shape armhole

Cast off 4 sts at beg of next row. 63 [65: 68: 70: 73] sts.

Dec 1 st at armhole edge of next 5 rows. 58 [60: 63: 65: 68] sts.

Cont straight until right front matches back to beg of shoulder shaping, ending with WS facing for next row.

Shape shoulder

Cast off 8 [8: 9: 9: 10] sts at beg of next and foll alt row, then 7 [8: 9: 10: 11] sts at beg of

foll alt row, ending with RS facing for
next row.

Break yarn and leave rem 35 [36: 36: 37: 37]
sts on a holder.

SLEEVES

Using 3¾mm (US 5) needles and yarn C, cast
on 56 [56: 58: 60: 60] sts.

Break off yarn C and join in yarn A.

Change to 4mm (US 6) needles.

Beg with a K row, work in st st, shaping sides
by inc 1 st at each end of 9th and every foll
8th row to 64 [64: 74: 66: 86] sts, then on
every foll 10th row until there are 80 [80: 84:
84: 88] sts.

Cont straight until sleeve meas 45 [45:
46: 46: 46] cm, ending with RS facing for
next row.

Shape top

Beg shaping top of sleeve as folls:

Cast off 4 sts at beg of next 2 rows. 72 [72:
76: 76: 80] sts.

Dec 1 st at each end of next and foll 3 alt
rows, then on foll row, ending with RS facing
for next row.

Cast off rem 62 [62: 66: 66: 70] sts.

MAKING UP

Press as described on the information page.
Join both shoulder seams using back stitch,
or mattress stitch if preferred.

Collar

With RS facing, using 4mm (US 6) needles
and yarn A, K 35 [36: 36: 37: 37] sts from
right front holder placing marker on last st,
pick up and knit 43 [45: 45: 47: 47] sts from
back, then K 35 [36: 36: 37: 37] sts from left
front holder placing marker on first st. 113
[117: 117: 121: 121] sts.

Work in moss st as given for back for 9 rows,
ending with RS facing for next row.

Row 10 (RS): *Moss st to within 1 st of
marked st, sl 1, work 2 tog (marked st is first
of these 2 sts), psso, rep from * once more,
moss st to end.

Work 7 rows.

Rep last 8 rows 3 times more, ending with
RS facing for next row. 97 [101: 101: 105:
105] sts.

Cast off in moss st.

See information page for finishing
instructions, setting in sleeves using the
shallow set-in method.

Crochet edging

Using 4.00mm (US G6) crochet hook and
yarn A, attach yarn at base of one side seam
and work one round of dc around entire
hem, front opening and collar edges,
working 3 dc into each corner point and
ending with ss to first dc, turn.

Next round: 1 ch (does NOT count as st),
1 dc into each dc to end, working 3 dc into
each corner point and ending with ss to
first dc.

Fasten off.

Work crochet edging around cast-on edges
of sleeves in same way.

DAPHNE SWEATER
Kaffe Fassett

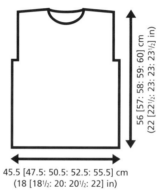

56 [57: 58: 59: 60] cm
(22 [22½: 23: 23: 23½] in)

45.5 [47.5: 50.5: 52.5: 55.5] cm
(18 [18½: 20: 20½: 22] in)

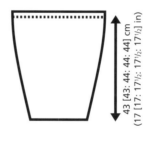

43 [43: 44: 44: 44] cm
(17 [17: 17½: 17½: 17½] in)

SIZES & YARNS

XS	S	M	L	XL	

To fit bust

81	86	91	97	102	cm
32	34	36	38	40	in

Rowan Scotttish Tweed DK and 4 ply
SWEATER

A DK Celtic mix 022

5	5	5	5	6	x 50gm

B DK Lavender 005

4	5	5	5	5	x 50gm

C 4 ply** Claret 013

3	3	3	3	3	x 25gm

D DK Apple 015

2	3	3	3	3	x 50gm

**Use 4 ply yarn doubled

NEEDLES

1 pair 3¼mm (no 10) (US 3) needles

1 pair 4mm (no 8) (US 6) needles

TENSION

20 sts and 28 rows to 10 cm measured over stocking stitch using 4mm (US 6) needles.

BACK

Using 3¼mm (US 3) needles and yarn A, cast on 91 [95: 101: 105: 111] sts.

Beg rib as folls:

Row 1 (RS): K1, *P1, K1, rep from * to end.

Row 2: P1, *K1, P1, rep from * to end.

These 2 rows form rib.

Work in rib for 1 row more, ending with WS facing for next row.

Change to 4mm (US 6) needles.

Row 4 (WS): Purl.

Beg and ending rows as indicated, using the intarsia technique as described on the information page and repeating the 40 row patt repeat throughout, cont in patt from chart, which is worked entirely in st st beg with a K row, as folls:

Cont in patt until back meas 36 [37: 37: 38:

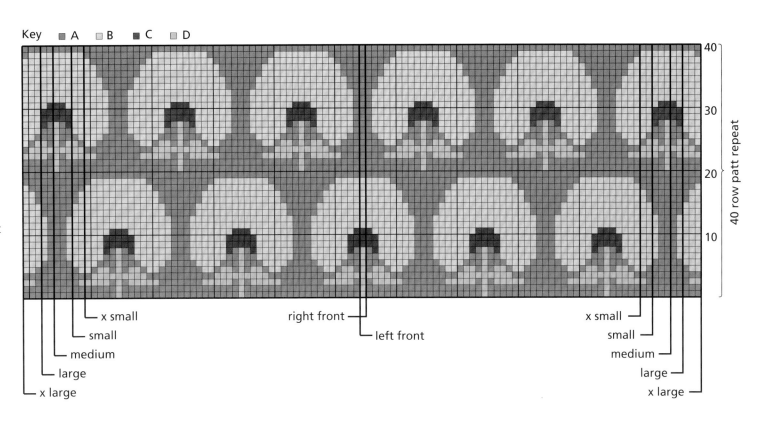

Key ■ A □ B ■ C □ D

40 row patt repeat

x small — small — medium — large — x large

right front — left front

x small — small — medium — large — x large

38] cm, ending with RS facing for next row.

Shape armholes

Keeping patt correct, cast off 5 sts at beg of next 2 rows. 81 [85: 91: 95: 101] sts.

Cont straight until armhole meas 20 [20: 21: 21: 22] cm, ending with RS facing for next row.

Shape shoulders and back neck

Cast off 8 [8: 9: 10: 11] sts at beg of next 2 rows. 65 [69: 73: 75: 79] sts.

Next row (RS): Cast off 8 [8: 9: 10: 11] sts, patt until there are 12 [13: 14: 13: 14] sts on right needle and turn, leaving rem sts on a holder.

Work each side of neck separately.

Cast off 4 sts at beg of next row.

Cast off rem 8 [9: 10: 9: 10] sts.

With RS facing, rejoin yarns to rem sts, cast off centre 25 [27: 27: 29: 29] sts, patt to end.

Complete to match first side, reversing shapings.

FRONT

Work as given for back until 16 [16: 16: 18: 18] rows less have been worked than on back to beg of shoulder shaping, ending with RS facing for next row.

Shape neck

Next row (RS): Patt 34 [35: 38: 40: 43] sts and turn, leaving rem sts on a holder.

Work each side of neck separately.

Cast off 4 sts at beg of next row. 30 [31: 34: 36: 39] sts.

Dec 1 st at neck edge of next 3 rows, then on foll 2 [2: 2: 3: 3] alt rows, then on foll 4th row. 24 [25: 28: 29: 32] sts.

Work 3 rows, ending with RS facing for next row.

Shape shoulder

Cast off 8 [8: 9: 10: 11] sts at beg of next and foll alt row.

Work 1 row.

Cast off rem 8 [9: 10: 9: 10] sts.

With RS facing, rejoin yarns to rem sts, cast off centre 13 [15: 15: 15: 15] sts, patt to end.

Complete to match first side, reversing shapings.

SLEEVE STRIPE SEQUENCE

Beg with a purl row, work in st st in stripes as folls:

Row 1: Using yarn A.

Rows 2 and 3: Using yarn D.

Row 4: Using yarn C.

Row 5: Using yarn A.

Row 6: Using yarn B.

Row 7: Using yarn C.

Rows 8 and 9: Using yarn A.

Row 10: Using yarn D.

Rows 11 to 13: Using yarn B.

Row 14: Using yarn C.

Rows 15 and 16: Using yarn D.

Rows 17 to 19: Using yarn A.

Rows 20 and 21: Using yarn B.

Rows 22 and 23: Using yarn D.

Row 24: Using yarn C.

Row 25: Using yarn A.

These 25 rows form stripe sequence for sleeve and should be repeated as required.

SLEEVES

Using 3¼mm (US 3) needles and yarn A, cast on 45 [45: 47: 49: 49] sts.

Work in rib as given for back for 3 rows, ending with WS facing for next row.

Change to 4mm (US 6) needles.

Beg with a P row, now work in st st in sleeve stripe sequence throughout (see above) and cont as folls:

Inc 1 st at each end of 6th [6th: 6th: 8th: 6th] and every foll 6th row to 79 [79: 81: 85: 79] sts, then on every foll 4th [4th: 4th: -: 4th] row until there are 81 [81: 85: -: 89] sts.

Cont straight until sleeve meas 46 [46: 47: 47: 47] cm, ending with RS facing for next row.

Cast off.

MAKING UP

Press as described on the information page (see page 97).

Join right shoulder seam using back stitch, or mattress stitch if preferred.

Neckband

With RS facing, using 3¼mm (US 3) needles and yarn A, pick up and knit 20 [20: 20: 22: 22] sts down left side of neck, 13 [15: 15: 15: 15] sts from front, 20 [20: 20: 22: 22] sts up right side of neck, then 32 [34: 34: 36: 36] sts from back. 85 [89: 89: 95: 95] sts.

Beg with row 2, work in rib as given for back for 3 rows, ending with RS facing for next row.

DAPHNE CARDIGAN
Kaffe Fassett

Cast off in rib.

See information page for finishing instructions, setting in sleeves using the square set-in method.

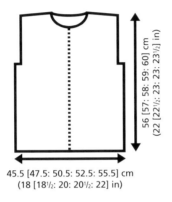

45.5 [47.5: 50.5: 52.5: 55.5] cm
(18 [18½: 20: 20½: 22] in)

56 [57: 58: 59: 60] cm
(22 [22½: 23: 23: 23½] in)

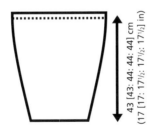

43 [43: 44: 44: 44] cm
(17 [17: 17½: 17½: 17½] in)

SIZES & YARNS

XS	S	M	L	XL	

To fit bust

| 81 | 86 | 91 | 97 | 102 | cm |
| 32 | 34 | 36 | 38 | 40 | in |

Rowan Harris Tweed DK and 4 ply

A DK Sunset 011

| 5 | 5 | 5 | 5 | 6 | x 50gm |

B DK Brill Pink 010

| 4 | 5 | 5 | 5 | 5 | x 50gm |

C 4 ply** Machair 002

| 3 | 3 | 3 | 3 | 3 | x 25gm |

D DK Apple 015

| 2 | 3 | 3 | 3 | 3 | x 50gm |

**Use 4 ply yarn doubled

NEEDLES

1 pair 3¼mm (no 10) (US 3) needles
1 pair 4mm (no 8) (US 6) needles

BUTTONS – 7 x Rowan No. 00324

TENSION

20 sts and 28 rows to 10 cm measured over stocking stitch using 4mm (US 6) needles.

BACK

Work as given for back of Daphne Sweater (see pages 45-6).

LEFT FRONT

Using 3¼mm (US 3) needles and yarn A, cast on 46 [48: 50: 52: 56] sts.
Beg rib as folls:
Row 1 (RS): *K1, P1, rep from * to end.
Row 2: As row 1.
These 2 rows form rib.
Work in rib for 1 row more, inc 0 [0: 1: 1: 0] st at beg of this row and ending with WS facing for next row. 46 [48: 51: 53: 56] sts.
Change to 4mm (US 6) needles.
Row 4 (WS): Purl.

Beg and ending rows as indicated, cont in patt from chart on page 45 as folls:

Cont in patt until left front matches back to beg of armhole shaping, ending with RS facing for next row.

Shape armhole

Keeping patt correct, cast off 5 sts at beg of next row. 41 [43: 46: 48: 51] sts.

Cont straight until 17 [17: 17: 19: 19] rows less have been worked than on back to beg of shoulder shaping, ending with WS facing for next row.

Shape neck

Keeping patt correct, cast off 7 [8: 8: 8: 8] sts at beg of next row, then 4 sts at beg of foll alt row. 30 [31: 34: 36: 39] sts.

Dec 1 st at neck edge of next 3 rows, then on foll 2 [2: 2: 3: 3] alt rows, then on foll 4th row. 24 [25: 28: 29: 32] sts.

Work 3 rows, ending with RS facing for next row.

Shape shoulder

Cast off 8 [8: 9: 10: 11] sts at beg of next and foll alt row.

Work 1 row.

Cast off rem 8 [9: 10: 9: 10] sts.

RIGHT FRONT

Using 3¼mm (US 3) needles and yarn A, cast on 46 [48: 50: 52: 56] sts.

Row 1 (RS): *P1, K1, rep from * to end.

Row 2: As row 1.

These 2 rows form rib.

Work in rib for 1 row more, inc 0 [0: 1: 1: 0] st at end of this row and ending with WS facing for next row. 46 [48: 51: 53: 56] sts.

Complete to match left front, reversing shapings.

SLEEVES

Work as given for sleeves of sweater.

MAKING UP

Press as described on the information page. Join both shoulder seams using back stitch, or mattress stitch if preferred.

Neckband

With RS facing, using 3¼mm (US 3) needles and yarn A, beg and ending at front opening edges, pick up and knit 27 [28: 28: 30: 30] sts up right side of neck, 33 [35: 35: 37: 37] sts from back, then 27 [28: 28: 30: 30] sts down left side of neck. 87 [91: 91: 97:

97] sts.

Beg with row 2, work in rib as given for back for 3 rows, ending with RS facing for next row.

Cast off in rib.

Button border

With RS facing, using 3¼mm (US 3) needles and yarn A, pick up and knit 103 [105: 107: 107: 109] sts evenly down left front opening edge, from top of neck border to cast-on edge.

Beg with row 2, work in rib as given for back for 3 rows, ending with RS facing for next row. Cast off in rib.

Buttonhole border

With RS facing, using 3¼mm (US 3) needles and yarn A, pick up and knit 103 [105: 107: 107: 109] sts evenly up right front opening edge, from cast-on edge to top of neck border.

Beg with row 2, work in rib as given for back for 1 row, ending with RS facing for next row.

Row 2 (RS): Rib 2 [3: 1: 1: 2], *work 2 tog, yrn (to make a buttonhole), rib 14 [14: 15: 15: 15], rep from * 5 times more, work

2 tog, yrn (to make 7th buttonhole), rib 3 [4: 2: 2: 3].

Work in rib for 1 row more, ending with RS facing for next row.

Cast off in rib.

See information page for finishing instructions, setting in sleeves using the square set-in method.

HOT STRIPE TOP
Sasha Kagan

SIZES & YARNS

	XS	S	M	L	XL	
To fit bust						
	81	86	91	97	102	cm
	32	34	36	38	40	in

Rowan Scottish Tweed 4 ply

	XS	S	M	L	XL	
A Midnight 023	4	4	5	5	5	x 25gm
B Rust 009	3	3	4	4	4	x 25gm
C Brill Pink 010	3	3	3	3	4	x 25gm
D Lewis Grey 007	3	3	3	3	3	x 25gm
E Sunset 011	2	2	2	2	2	x 25gm
F Storm Grey 004	3	3	3	3	3	x 25gm
G Thatch 018	2	2	2	2	2	x 25gm
H Grey Mist 001	3	3	3	3	3	x 25gm
J Thistle 016	1	1	1	1	1	x 25gm

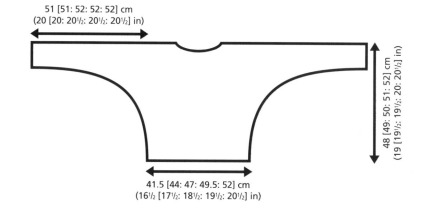

51 [51: 52: 52: 52] cm
(20 [20: 20½: 20½: 20½] in)

48 [49: 50: 51: 52] cm
(19 [19½: 19½: 20: 20½] in)

41.5 [44: 47: 49.5: 52] cm
(16½ [17½: 18½: 19½: 20½] in)

NEEDLES

1 pair 2¾mm (no 12) (US 2) needles

1 pair 3¼mm (no 10) (US 3) needles

3mm (no 11) (US 2-3) circular needle

TENSION

26 sts and 38 rows to 10 cm measured over rib when pressed using 3¼mm (US 3) needles.

STRIPE SEQUENCE

Work in rib in stripes as folls:

Rows 1 and 2: Using yarn G.

Rows 3 and 4: Using yarn A.

Rows 5 to 7: Using yarn C.

Rows 8 and 9: Using yarn H.

Rows 10 and 11: Using yarn E.

Rows 12 to 14: Using yarn F.

Rows 15 and 16: Using yarn A.

Rows 17 and 18: Using yarn C.

Rows 19 and 20: Using yarn B.

Rows 21 to 23: Using yarn A.

Rows 24 to 26: Using yarn D.

Rows 27 and 28: Using yarn E.

Rows 29 and 30: Using yarn F.

Rows 31 to 33: Using yarn A.

Rows 34 and 35: Using yarn J.

Rows 36 and 37: Using yarn C.

Rows 38 and 39: Using yarn E.

Rows 40 to 42: Using yarn G.

Rows 43 and 44: Using yarn E.

Rows 45 and 46: Using yarn C.

Rows 47 and 48: Using yarn J.

Rows 49 to 51: Using yarn A.

Rows 52 and 53: Using yarn B.

Rows 54 and 55: Using yarn C.

Rows 56 and 57: Using yarn B.

Rows 58 to 60: Using yarn F.

Rows 61 to 63: Using yarn G.

Rows 64 to 66: Using yarn A.

Rows 67 to 69: Using yarn C.

Rows 70 and 71: Using yarn F.

Rows 72 and 73: Using yarn E.

Rows 74 to 76: Using yarn D.

Rows 77 and 78: Using yarn A.

Rows 79 and 80: Using yarn C.

Rows 81 and 82: Using yarn B.

Rows 83 to 85: Using yarn A.

Rows 86 and 87: Using yarn B.

Rows 88 and 89: Using yarn C.

Rows 90 and 91: Using yarn A.

Rows 92 to 94: Using yarn D.

Rows 95 and 96: Using yarn E.

Rows 97 and 98: Using yarn F.

Rows 99 to 101: Using yarn C.

Rows 102 and 103: Using yarn A.

Rows 104 to 106: Using yarn G.

Rows 107 to 111: Using yarn F.

Rows 112 and 113: Using yarn B.

Rows 114 and 115: Using yarn C.

Rows 116 and 117: Using yarn B.

Rows 118 to 122: Using yarn H.

Rows 123 and 124: Using yarn G.

Rows 125 and 126: Using yarn E.

Rows 127 and 128: Using yarn C.

Rows 129 and 130: Using yarn J.

Rows 131 and 132: Using yarn C.

Rows 133 and 134: Using yarn E.

Rows 135 and 136: Using yarn G.

Rows 137 to 141: Using yarn H.

Rows 142 and 143: Using yarn B.

Rows 144 and 145: Using yarn C.

Rows 146 and 147: Using yarn B.

Rows 148 to 153: Using yarn A.

Rows 154 and 155: Using yarn G.

Rows 156 and 157: Using yarn F.

Rows 158 to 160: Using yarn E.

Rows 161 and 162: Using yarn D.

Rows 163 and 164: Using yarn H.

Rows 165 and 166: Using yarn D.

Rows 167 and 168: Using yarn E.

Rows 169 and 170: Using yarn F.

Rows 171 and 172: Using yarn G.

Rows 173 to 177: Using yarn A.

Rows 178 and 179: Using yarn C.

Rows 180 and 181: Using yarn A.

Rows 182 and 183: Using yarn B.

Rows 184 and 185: Using yarn D.

Rows 186 and 187: Using yarn H.

Rows 188 and 189: Using yarn E.

Rows 190 and 191: Using yarn H.

Rows 192 and 193: Using yarn D.

Rows 194 and 195: Using yarn B.

Rows 196 and 197: Using yarn A.

Rows 198 and 199: Using yarn C.

Rows 200 to 203: Using yarn A.

Rows 204 and 205: Using yarn G.

Rows 206 and 207: Using yarn H.

Rows 208 to 210: Using yarn E.

Rows 211 and 212: Using yarn B.

Rows 213 and 214: Using yarn J.

Rows 215 and 216: Using yarn B.

Rows 217 to 219: Using yarn E.

Rows 220 and 221: Using yarn H.

Rows 222 and 223: Using yarn G.

Rows 224 to 228: Using yarn A.

Rows 229 and 230: Using yarn B.

Rows 231 and 232: Using yarn C.

Rows 233 and 234: Using yarn B.

Rows 235 to 242: Using yarn H.

Rows 243 and 244: Using yarn J.

Rows 245 and 246: Using yarn C.

Rows 247 and 248: Using yarn E.

Rows 249 and 250: Using yarn G.

Rows 251 and 252: Using yarn E.

Rows 253 and 254: Using yarn C.

Rows 255 and 256: Using yarn J.

Rows 257 and 264: Using yarn H.

Rows 265 and 266: Using yarn B.

Rows 267 and 268: Using yarn C.

Rows 269 and 270: Using yarn B.

Rows 271 to 275: Using yarn F.

Rows 276 to 278: Using yarn G.

Rows 279 and 280: Using yarn A.

Rows 281 to 283: Using yarn C.

Rows 284 and 285: Using yarn F.

Rows 286 and 287: Using yarn E.

Rows 288 to 290: Using yarn D.

Rows 291 and 292: Using yarn A.

Rows 293 and 294: Using yarn C.

Rows 295 and 296: Using yarn B.

Rows 297 and 298: Using yarn A.

At this point, you will have reached the centre front/back of the garment. Work the stripes on the remainder of the garment in reverse, so that they form a mirror image, by working rows 297 and 298 again, then rows 295 and 296, then rows 293 and 294, and so on.

BODY

The body is worked in one piece from cuff to cuff.

Using 3¼mm (US 3) needles and yarn D [A: E: C: G], cast on 62 [62: 64: 66: 66] sts.

Beg with stripe sequence row 25 [21: 11: 7: 1], now cont in stripe sequence throughout (see above) as folls:

Row 1 (RS): P0 [0: 1: 2: 2], *K6, P2, rep from * to last 6 [6: 7: 8: 8] sts, K6, P0 [0: 1: 2: 2].

Row 2: K0 [0: 1: 2: 2], *P6, K2, rep from * to last 6 [6: 7: 8: 8] sts, P6, K0 [0: 1: 2: 2].

These 2 rows form rib.

Work a further 8 [8: 12: 12: 12] rows, ending with RS facing for next row.

Inc 1 st at each end of next and every foll 10th row to 70 [70: 72: 74: 74] sts, then on every foll 6th row to 76 [76: 78: 80: 80] sts, then on every foll 4th row to 128 [128: 130: 132: 132] sts, then on foll 8 alt rows, then on foll 9 rows, taking inc sts into rib and ending with RS facing for next row. 162 [162: 164: 166: 166] sts.

Shape side seam

Cast on 8 sts at beg of next 6 rows, then 12 [14: 16: 17: 20] sts at beg of foll 2 rows. 234 [238: 244: 248: 254] sts.

Work 42 [46: 50: 54: 58] rows, ending with RS facing for next row.

Shape neck

Next row (RS): Rib 114 [116: 119: 121: 124] and turn, leaving rem sts on a holder.

Work each side of neck separately.

**Keeping stripes correct, dec 1 st at neck edge of next 4 rows, then on foll 2 alt rows, then on every foll 4th row until 105 [107: 110: 112: 115] sts rem.

Work 31 [31: 35: 35: 39] rows, ending with RS facing for next row.

Inc 1 st at neck edge of next and every foll 4th row to 109 [111: 114: 116: 119] sts,

then on foll 2 alt rows, then on foll 3 rows, ending with RS facing for next row. 114 [116: 119: 121: 124] sts.**

Break yarn and leave these sts on a second holder.

With RS facing, rejoin yarn to rem sts, cast off centre 6 sts, rib to end. 114 [116: 119: 121: 124] sts.

Work from ** to ** once more.

Break yarn.

Join sections

Next row (RS): Rib across 114 [116: 119: 121: 124] sts of first section left on holder, turn and cast on 6 sts, rib across 114 [116: 119: 121: 124] sts of second section. 234 [238: 244: 248: 254] sts.

Work 43 [47: 51: 55: 59] rows, ending with RS facing for next row.

Shape side seam

Keeping stripes correct, cast off 13 [15: 17: 18: 21] sts at beg of next 2 rows, then 8 sts at beg of foll 6 rows. 160 [160: 162: 164: 164] sts.

Dec 1 st at each end of next 8 rows, then on foll 9 alt rows, then on every foll 4th row to 74 [74: 76: 78: 78] sts, then on every foll 6th row to 68 [68: 70: 72: 72] sts, then on every foll 10th row until 62 [62: 64: 66: 66] sts rem.

Work 8 [8: 12: 12: 12] rows, ending with RS facing for next row.

Cast off in rib, using same colour as for previous row.

MAKING UP

Press as described on the information page.

Hem borders (both alike)

With RS facing, using 2¾mm (US 2) needles and yarn A, pick up and knit 122 [126: 134: 138: 146] sts evenly across row-end edge between side seam shaping.

Row 1 (WS): P2, *K2, P2, rep from * to end.
Row 2: K2, *P2, K2, rep from * to end.
These 2 rows form rib.

Work in rib for a further 8 rows, ending with WS facing for next row.

Cast off in rib (on WS).

Collar

With RS facing, using 3mm (US 2-3) circular needle and yarn A, beg and ending at centre back neck, pick up and knit 124 [128: 132: 136: 140] sts evenly all round neck edge.

Round 1 (RS): *K2, P2, rep from * to end.
This round forms rib.
Work in rib until collar meas 22 cm.
Cast off in rib.

Join underarm and side seams using back stitch, or mattress stitch if preferred.

BACKGAMMON SWEATER AND SLIPOVER
Kaffe Fassett

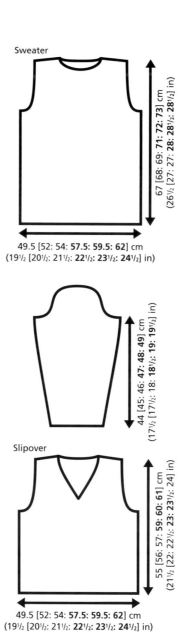

Sweater

67 [68: 69: **71: 72: 73**] cm
(26½ [27: 27: **28: 28½: 28½**] in)

49.5 [52: 54: **57.5: 59.5: 62**] cm
(19½ [20½: 21½: **22½: 23½: 24½**] in)

44 [45: 46: **47: 48: 49**] cm
(17½ [17½: 17½: **18: 18½: 19½**] in)

Slipover

55 [56: 57: **59: 60: 61**] cm
(21½ [22: 22½: **23: 23½: 24**] in)

49.5 [52: 54: **57.5: 59.5: 62**] cm
(19½ [20½: 21½: **22½: 23½: 24½**] in)

SIZES & YARNS

women's			men's			
S	M	L	M	L	XL	

To fit bust/chest

| 86 | 91 | 97 | 102 | 107 | 112 | cm |
| 34 | 36 | 38 | 40 | 42 | 44 | in |

Rowan ScottishTweed 4 ply
Slipover

	S	M	L	M	L	XL	
A Herring 008	5	6	6	6	7	7	x 25gm
B Lobster 017	1	1	1	1	1	1	x 25gm
C Winter Navy 021	1	1	1	1	1	1	x 25gm
D Celtic Mix 022	1	1	1	1	1	1	x 25gm
E Rust 009	1	1	1	1	1	1	x 25gm
F Apple 015	1	1	1	1	1	1	x 25gm
G Peat 019	1	1	1	1	1	1	x 25gm

Sweater

A Midnight 023

10	11	11	12	13	14	x 25gm

B Mallard 020

1	1	1	1	1	2	x 25gm

C Lewis Grey 007

2	2	2	2	2	2	x 25gm

D Celtic Mix 022

2	2	2	2	2	2	x 25gm

E Peat 019

2	2	2	2	2	2	x 25gm

F Claret 013

2	2	2	2	2	2	x 25gm

G Heath 014

2	2	2	2	2	2	x 25gm

NEEDLES

1 pair 2¾mm (no 12) (US 2) needles
1 pair 3¼mm (no 10) (US 3) needles
2¾mm (no 12) (US 2) circular needle

TENSION

26 sts and 38 rows to 10 cm measured over patterned stocking stitch using 3¼mm (US 3) needles.

Pattern note: The pattern is written for three women's sizes, followed by three men's sizes in **bold**. Where only one figure appears this applies to all sizes in that group. Take special care to follow chosen size throughout.

SWEATER

BACK

Using 2¾mm (US 2) needles and yarn A, cast on 128 [133: 143: **148: 153: 163**] sts.
Row 1 (RS): K3, *P2, K3, rep from * to end.
Row 2: P3, *K2, P3, rep from * to end.
These 2 rows form rib.
Work in rib for a further 22 rows, inc [inc: dec: **inc: inc: dec**] 1 [2: 2: **1: 2: 2**] sts evenly across last row and ending with RS facing for next row. 129 [135: 141: **149: 155: 161**] sts. Change to 3¼mm (US 3) needles.**
Beg and ending rows as indicated and using the intarsia technique as described on the information page (see page 96), cont in patt from chart for sweater body, which is worked entirely in st st beg with a K row, as folls:
Work straight until chart row 156 [**160**] has been completed, ending with RS facing for next row. (Back should meas 47 [**48**] cm.)

Shape armholes

Keeping chart correct, cast off 6 [7: 8: **9: 10: 11**] sts at beg of next 2 rows. 117 [121: 125: **131: 135: 139**] sts.
Dec 1 st at each end of next 5 [5: 7: **7: 9: 9**] rows, then on foll 1 [2: 1: **2: 1: 2**] alt rows, then on every foll 4th row until 101 [103: 105: **109: 111: 113**] sts rem.
Cont straight until chart row 232 [236: 240: **248: 252: 256**] has been completed, ending with RS facing for next row.
(Armhole should meas 20 [21: 22: **23: 24: 25**] cm.)

Shape shoulders and back neck

Cast off 9 [9: 10: **10**] sts at beg of next 2 rows. 83 [85: 85: **89: 91: 93**] sts.
Next row (RS): Cast off 9 [9: 10: **10**] sts, K until there are 14 [14: 13: **14: 15: 15**] sts on right needle and turn, leaving rem sts on a holder.
Work each side of neck separately.
Cast off 4 sts at beg of next row.
Cast off rem 10 [10: 9: **10: 11: 11**] sts.
With RS facing, rejoin appropriate yarns to rem sts, cast off centre 37 [39: 39: **41: 41: 43**] sts, K to end.
Complete to match first side, reversing shapings.

FRONT

Work as given for back until 22 [**24**] rows less have been worked than on back to beg of shoulder shaping, ending with RS facing for next row.

Shape neck

Next row (RS): K42 [42: 43: **45: 46: 46**] and turn, leaving rem sts on a holder.
Work each side of neck separately.
Cast off 5 sts at beg of next row. 37 [37: 38: **40: 41: 41**] sts.
Dec 1 st at neck edge of next 5 rows, then on foll 2 [**3**] alt rows, then on every foll 4th row until 28 [28: 29: **30: 31: 31**] sts rem.
Work 3 rows, ending with RS facing for next row.

Shape shoulder

Cast off 9 [9: 10: **10**] sts at beg of next and foll alt row.
Work 1 row.
Cast off rem 10 [10: 9: **10: 11: 11**] sts.

Sweater body chart

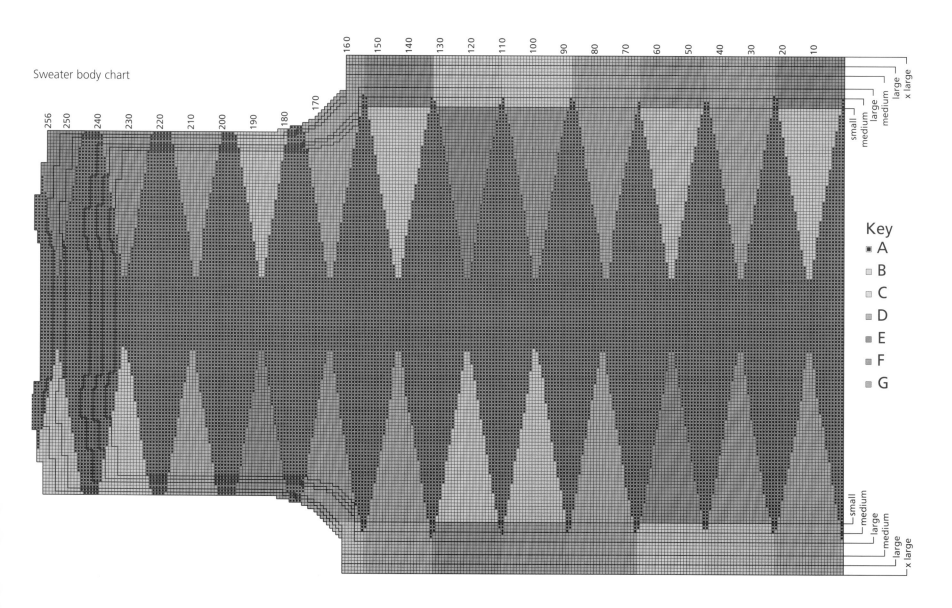

Key
A
B
C
D
E
F
G

Slipover chart

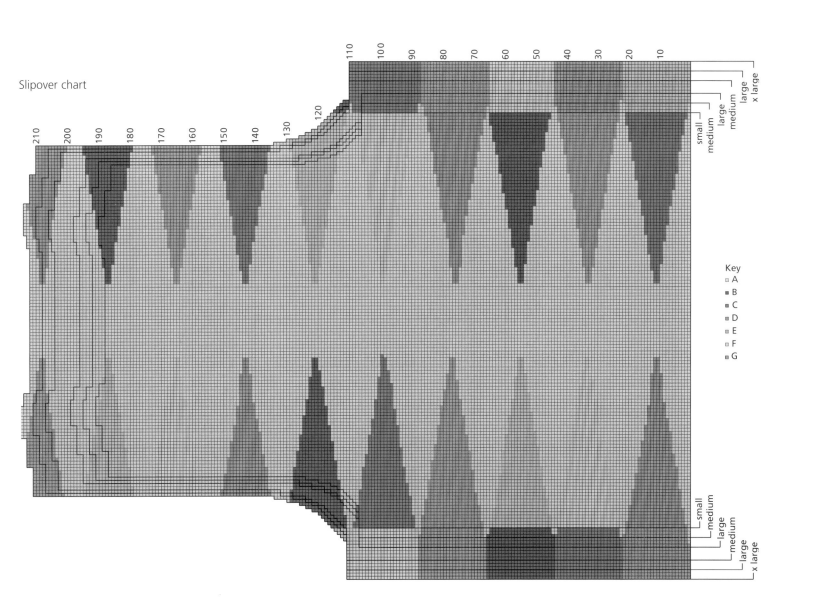

Key
☐ A
■ B
■ C
■ D
■ E
☐ F
■ G

Sleeve chart

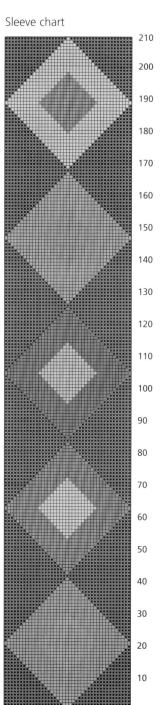

With RS facing, rejoin appropriate yarns to rem sts, cast off centre 17 [19: 19: **19: 19: 21**] sts, K to end.

Complete to match first side, reversing shapings.

SLEEVES

Using 2¾mm (US 2) needles and yarn A, cast on 58 [63: 63: **63: 63: 68**] sts.

Work in rib as given for back for 24 rows, inc [dec: -: -: **inc: dec**] 1 [2: -: -: **2: 1**] sts evenly across last row and ending with RS facing for next row. 59 [61: 63: **63: 65: 67**] sts.

Change to 3¼mm (US 3) needles.

Place chart

Place chart as folls:

Row 1 (RS): Using yarn A K9 [10: 11: **11: 12: 13**], work next 41 sts as row 1 of chart for sleeve, using yarn A K to end.

Row 2: Using yarn A P9 [10: 11: **11: 12: 13**], work next 41 sts as row 2 of chart for sleeve, using yarn A P to end.

These 2 rows set position of chart with edge sts in st st using yarn A.

(**Note:** On larger sizes, chart will end before top of sleeve. Once all 210 rows of chart have been worked, complete sleeve by working sts above chart in st st using yarn A.)

Keeping chart correct, cont as folls:

Inc 1 st at each end of 3rd [**next**] and every foll 6th [**4th**] row to 71 [85: 99: **71: 81: 91**] sts, then on every foll 8th [**6th**] row until there are 93 [99: 105: **111: 117: 123**] sts, taking inc sts into st st using yarn A.

Cont straight until sleeve meas 44 [45: 46: **47: 48: 49**] cm, ending with RS facing for next row.

Shape top

Keeping chart correct, cast off 6 [7: 8: **9: 10: 11**] sts at beg of next 2 rows. 81 [85: 89: **93: 97: 101**] sts.

Dec 1 st at each end of next 5 rows, then on foll 2 alt rows, then on every foll 4th row until 61 [65: 69: **63: 67: 71**] sts rem.

Work 1 row.

Dec 1 st at each end of next and every foll alt row until 47 [**57**] sts rem, then on foll 7 rows, ending with RS facing for next row. 33 [**43**] sts.

Cast off 5 [**10**] sts at beg of next 2 rows.

Cast off rem 23 sts.

MAKING UP

Press as described on the information page. Join right shoulder seam using back stitch, or mattress stitch if preferred.

Neckband

With RS facing, using 2¾mm (US 2) needles and yarn A, pick up and knit 26 [**28**] sts down left side of neck, 17 [19: 19: **19: 19: 21**] sts from front, 26 [**28**] sts up right side of neck, then 44 [47: 47: **48: 48: 51**] sts from back. 113 [118: 118: **123: 123: 128**] sts.

Beg with row 2, work in rib as given for back for 8 cm.

Cast off in rib.

See information page for finishing instructions, setting in sleeves using the set-in method.

SLIPOVER

BACK

Work as given for back of sweater to **.
Beg and ending rows as indicated and using the intarsia technique as described on the information page, cont in patt from chart for slipover, which is worked entirely in st st beg with a K row, as folls:

Work straight until chart row 106 [**110**] has been completed, ending with RS facing for next row. (Back should meas 34 [**35**] cm.)

Shape armholes

Keeping chart correct, cast off 7 [8: 9: **10: 11: 12**] sts at beg of next 2 rows. 115 [119: 123: **129: 133: 137**] sts.

Dec 1 st at each end of next 5 [5: 7: **7: 9: 9**] rows, then on foll 2 [3: 2: **3: 2: 3**] alt rows, then on every foll 4th row until 97 [99: 101: **105: 107: 109**] sts rem.***

Cont straight until chart row 186 [190: 194: **202: 206: 210**] has been completed, ending with RS facing for next row. (Armhole should meas 21 [22: 23: **24: 25: 26**] cm.)

Shape shoulders and back neck

Cast off 8 [8: 9: **9**] sts at beg of next 2 rows. 81 [83: 83: **87: 89: 91**] sts.

Next row (RS): Cast off 8 [8: 9: **9**] sts, K until there are 13 [13: 12: **13: 14: 14**] sts on right needle and turn, leaving rem sts on a holder.

Work each side of neck separately.

Cast off 4 sts at beg of next row.

Cast off rem 9 [9: 8: **9: 10: 10**] sts.

With RS facing, rejoin appropriate yarns to rem sts, cast off centre 39 [41: 41: **43: 43: 45**] sts, K to end.

Complete to match first side, reversing shapings.

FRONT

Work as given for back to ***.

Work 1 row, ending with RS facing for next row.

Divide for neck

Next row (RS): K48 [49: 50: **52: 53: 54**] and turn, leaving rem sts on a holder.

Work each side of neck separately.

Dec 1 st at neck edge of 2nd and foll 21 [22: 20: **21: 19: 20**] alt rows, then on every foll 4th row until 25 [25: 26: **27: 28: 28**] sts rem.

Cont straight until front matches back to beg of shoulder shaping, ending with RS facing for next row.

Shape shoulder

Cast off 8 [8: 9: **9**] sts at beg of next and foll alt row.

Work 1 row.

Cast off rem 9 [9: 8: **9: 10: 10**] sts.

With RS facing, rejoin appropriate yarns to rem sts, K2tog, K to end. 48 [49: 50: **52: 53: 54**] sts.

Complete to match first side, reversing shapings.

MAKING UP

Press as described on the information page. Join both shoulder seams using back stitch, or mattress stitch if preferred.

Neckband

With RS facing, using 2¾mm (US 2) circular needle and yarn A, pick up and knit 56 [56: 61: **61: 66: 66**] sts down left side of neck, 1 st from base of V (mark this st with a coloured thread), 56 [56: 61: **61: 66: 66**] sts up right side of neck, then 47 [**52**] sts from back. 160 [160: 170: **175: 185: 185**] sts.

Round 1 (RS): *K3, P2, rep from * to end.
This round sets position of rib.
Keeping rib correct, cont as folls:

Round 2: Rib to within 2 sts of marked st, K2tog, K marked st, K2tog tbl, rib to end.

Round 3: Rib to within 1 st of marked st, K3 (marked st is centre st of these 3 sts), rib to end.

Rep last 2 rounds 3 times more. 152 [152: 162: **167: 177: 177**] sts.

Cast off in rib, still dec 1 st at either side of marked st as before.

Armhole borders (both alike)

With RS facing, using 2¾mm (US 2) needles and yarn A, pick up and knit 123 [128: 138: **143: 153: 158**] sts evenly all round armhole edge.

Beg with row 2, work in rib as given for back for 10 rows, ending with WS facing for next row.

Cast off in rib (on WS).

See information page for finishing instructions, setting in sleeves using the set-in method.

MAYA BATWING TOP AND SNOOD
Di Gilpin

SIZES & YARNS

S-L (one size fits all)

To fit bust
86-97 cm
34-38 in

Rowan Scottish Tweed Aran
Sweater: 5 x 100gm
Snood: 1 x 100gm
(photographed in Rust 009)

NEEDLES

1 pair 5mm (no 6) (US 8) needles
Sweater: 1 pair 4mm (no 8) (US 6) needles,
and 4mm (no 8) (US 6) circular needle
Snood: 1 pair 4½mm (no 7) (US 7) needles

EXTRAS

Sweater only: 7 m of leather thonging

TENSION

16 sts and 23 rows to 10 cm measured over
stocking stitch using 5mm (US 8) needles.

SPECIAL ABBREVIATION

MB = make bobble as folls: (K1, yfwd, K1,
yfwd, K1) all into next st, turn, P5, turn,
K5, turn, P2tog, P1, P2tog tbl, turn, sl 1,
K2tog, psso.

SWEATER
BODY

The body is worked in one piece from cuff
to cuff.
Using 4mm (US 6) needles, cast on 44 sts.
Beg moss st as folls:
Row 1 (RS): *K1, P1, rep from * to end.
Row 2: *P1, K1, rep from * to end.
These 2 rows form moss st.
Row 3: Moss st 2 sts, *MB, moss st 7 sts,
rep from * to last 2 sts, MB, moss st 1 st.
Row 4: *P3tog, moss st 5 sts, rep from * to
last 4 sts, P3tog, moss st 1 st. 32 sts.
Work in moss st for a further 2 rows.
Row 7: Moss st 4 sts, *MB, moss st 5 sts,
rep from * to last 4 sts, MB, moss st 3 sts.
Work in moss st for a further 3 rows, inc 1 st
at each end of last row and ending with RS
facing for next row. 34 sts.
Change to 5mm (US 8) needles.

Cont in patt from chart as folls:

Inc 1 st at each end of 9th and every foll 8th row to 42 sts, then on every foll 6th row to 50 sts, then on every foll 4th row to 58 sts, then on foll 9 alt rows, then on foll 7 rows, ending with RS facing for next row. 90 sts.

Shape left side seam

Keeping chart correct, cast on 22 sts at beg of next 2 rows. 134 sts.

Work 32 rows, ending with RS facing for next row.

Shape back

Next row (RS): Patt 66 sts and turn, leaving rem sts on a holder.

Work each side of neck separately.

Keeping chart correct, dec 1 st at neck edge of 2nd and foll alt row, then on every foll 4th row until 61 sts rem.

Work 13 rows, ending with RS facing for next row.

Inc 1 st at neck edge of next and every foll 4th row to 65 sts, then on foll alt row. 66 sts.

Work 1 row, ending with RS facing for next row.

Leave these sts on a second holder but do NOT break off yarn.

Shape front

With RS facing, rejoin yarn to rem sts, cast off centre 4 sts, patt to end. 64 sts.

Keeping chart correct, dec 1 st at neck edge of 2nd and foll 4 alt rows, then on every foll 4th row until 57 sts rem.

Work 9 rows, ending with RS facing for next row.

Inc 1 st at neck edge of next and every foll 4th row to 60 sts, then on foll 4 alt rows. 64 sts.

Work 1 row, ending with RS facing for next row.

Break yarn.

Join sections

Next row (RS): Patt across 66 sts of back, turn and cast on 4 sts, patt across 64 sts of front. 134 sts.

Work 34 rows, ending with RS facing for next row.

Shape right side seam

Keeping chart correct, cast off 22 sts at beg of next 2 rows. 90 sts.

Dec 1 st at each end of next 8 rows, then on foll 9 alt rows, then on every foll 4th row to 48 sts, then on every foll 6th row to 40 sts, then on every foll 8th row until 34 sts rem.

Work 7 rows, ending with RS facing for next row.

Change to 4mm (US 6) needles.

Work in moss st as given for left cuff, dec 1 st at each end of first of these rows and ending with RS facing for next row.

Next row (RS): As row 7.

Work 2 rows.

Next row (WS): *Inc twice in next st, moss st 5 sts, rep from * to last 2 sts, inc twice in next st, moss st 1 st. 44 sts.

Next row: As row 3.

Work in moss st for a further 3 rows, ending with RS facing for next row.

Cast off in moss st.

MAKING UP

Press as described on the information page.

Neckband

With RS facing and using 4mm (US 6) circular needle, beg and ending at centre back neck, pick up and knit 85 sts evenly all round neck edge.

Round 1 (RS): Knit.

Round 2: Purl.

Cast off knitwise.

Cut thonging into 2 equal lengths. Using photograph as a guide, thread thonging through underarm and side seam edges to lace up these edges, tying ends at body hem edges.

SNOOD

Actual Measurement – 51 cm x 17 cm (20in x 6½in)

Using 4½mm (US 7) needles, cast on 82 sts.

Cont in patt from chart as folls:

Work 8 rows, ending with RS facing for next row.

Change to 5mm (US 8) needles.

Cont straight until chart row 36 has been completed, ending with RS facing for next row.

Change to 4½mm (US 7) needles.

Work a further 8 rows, ending after chart row 44 and with RS facing for next row.

Cast off in moss st.

MAKING UP

Press as described on the information page.

Join back seam using back stitch, or mattress stitch if preferred.

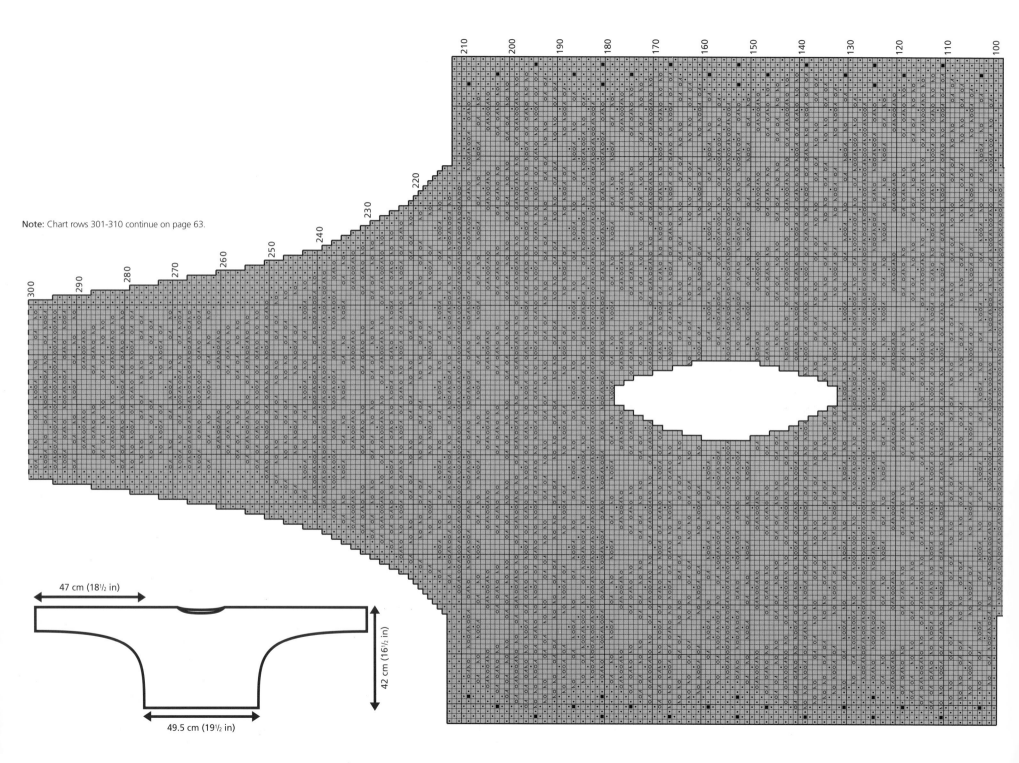

Note: Chart rows 301-310 continue on page 63.

47 cm (18½ in)

49.5 cm (19½ in)

42 cm (16½ in)

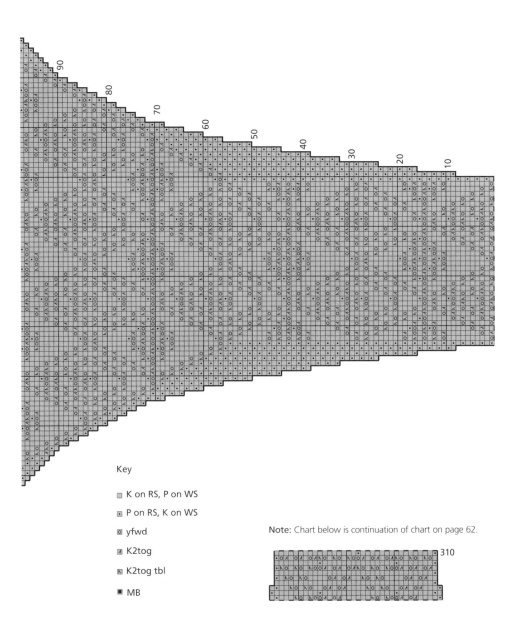

Key

- ⬜ K on RS, P on WS
- ⊡ P on RS, K on WS
- ⊙ yfwd
- ◩ K2tog
- ◨ K2tog tbl
- ◼ MB

Note: Chart below is continuation of chart on page 62.

310

Snood

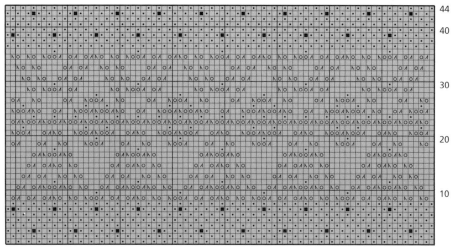

NESSIE BAG
Sarah Hatton

SIZE & YARNS

Rowan Scottish Tweed Aran

A Lavender 005

4 x 100gm

B Thistle 016

1 x 100gm

C Brill Pink 010

1 x 100gm

NEEDLES

1 pair 4mm (no 8) (US 6) needles

1 pair 4½mm (no 7) (US 7) needles

EXTRAS

Piece of lining fabric 91 cm (36 in) wide
and 40 cm (16 in) long

FINISHED SIZE

Completed bag measures approx 39 cm
(15½ in) wide and 25 cm (10 in) deep after
washing and felting.

TENSION

17 sts and 24 rows to 10 cm measured over
stocking stitch using 4½mm (US 7) needles.

MAIN SECTION

Using 4½mm (US 7) needles and yarn A, cast
on 68 sts.

Beg with a K row, work in st st for 32 cm,
ending with WS facing for next row.

Next row (WS): Knit (to form first base
fold line).

Beg with a K row, cont in st st for a
further 23 rows, ending with WS facing for
next row.

Next row (WS): Knit (to form second base
fold line).

Beg with a K row, cont in st st until work
meas 32 cm from second fold line row,
ending with WS facing for next row.

Next row (WS): Knit (to form flap fold line).

Beg with a K row and joining in and breaking
off colours as required, cont in striped st st
as folls:

Rows 1 to 6: Using yarn B.

Rows 7 and 8: Using yarn C.

Rows 9 to 12: Using yarn B.

Rows 13 and 14: Using yarn C.

Rows 15 to 28: As rows 1 to 14.

Rows 29 to 44: Using yarn A.

Rows 45 and 46: Using yarn C.

Rows 47 to 50: Using yarn B.

Rows 51 and 52: Using yarn C.

Cast off.

STRAP AND GUSSET

Using 4½mm (US 7) needles and yarn A, cast on 17 sts.

Beg with a K row, work in st st until strap meas 170 cm, ending with RS facing for next row.

Cast off.

BOBBLES (MAKE 4)

Using 4mm (US 6) needles and yarn B, cast on 3 sts.

Row 1 (RS): K1, yfwd, K1, yfwd, K1. 5 sts.

Row 2: P5.

Row 3: K5.

Row 4: P5.

Row 5: K1, sl 1, K2tog, psso, K1. 3 sts.

Row 6: P3tog and fasten off.

MAKING UP

Press as described on the information page.
Using photograph as a guide and yarn DOUBLE, work embroidery onto striped flap of main section as folls: Using yarn C, work lines of running stitch along each 4 row stripe using yarn B. Form each bobble into a ball and attach to flap section in yarn A as in photograph. Using yarn C, embroider 5 lazy daisy stitches around base of each bobble. Sew cast-on and cast-off edges of strap and gusset to row-end edges of main section between base fold line rows, then sew row-end edges together below flap fold line row and cast-on edge.

Hot machine wash at 60°C (to shrink and felt knitted pieces). Leave to dry, laid flat, then press following instructions on information page (see page 97).

Cut 2 pieces of lining fabric 41 cm wide and 27 cm long for sides, and one piece 91 cm wide and 11 cm long for gusset. Allowing 1 cm for seams, sew long edges of gusset to three edges of each side piece, leaving top edge open. Fold 1 cm to WS around top of lining. Slip lining inside bag and sew top edge in place.

RIPPLE SWEATER
Brandon Mably

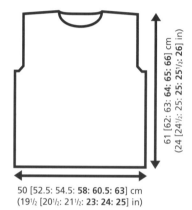

61 [62: 63: **64**: 65: **66**] cm
(24 [24½: 25: **25**: 25½: **26**] in)

50 [52.5: 54.5: **58**: 60.5: **63**] cm
(19½ [20½: 21½: **23**: 24: **25**] in)

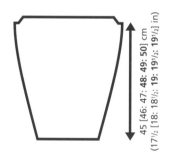

45 [46: 47: **48**: 49: **50**] cm
(17½ [18: 18½: **19**: 19½: **19½**] in)

SIZES & YARNS

women's			men's			
S	M	L	M	L	XL	

To fit bust/chest

86	91	97	102	107	112	cm
34	36	38	40	42	44	in

*Rowan Scottish Tweed 4 ply

A Grey Mist 001

4	4	4	4	4	5	x 25gm

B Lavender 005

5	5	5	6	6	6	x 25gm

C Skye 003

4	4	4	5	5	5	x 25gm

D Porridge 024

3	3	4	4	4	4	x 25gm

E Sea Green 006

4	4	4	4	5	5	x 25gm

F Machair 002

3	3	3	3	4	4	x 25gm

*Use yarn DOUBLE throughout.

NEEDLES

1 pair 4mm (no 8) (US 6) needles

1 pair 5mm (no 6) (US 8) needles

TENSION

17 sts and 21 rows to 10 cm measured over stocking stitch using 5mm (US 8) needles and yarn DOUBLE.

Pattern note: The pattern is written for three women's sizes, followed by three men's sizes in **bold**. Where only one figure appears this applies to all sizes in that group.

STRIPE SEQUENCE A

Beg with a K row and using all yarns DOUBLE, work in st st in stripes as folls:

Rows 1 to 4: Using yarn D.

Rows 5 to 11: Using yarn B.

Rows 12 to 16: Using yarn F.

Rows 17 to 22: Using yarn C.

Rows 23 to 27: Using yarn A.

Rows 28 to 32: Using yarn B.

Rows 33 to 39: Using yarn D.

Rows 40 to 43: Using yarn A.

Rows 44 to 49: Using yarn C.

Rows 50 to 57: Using yarn B.

Rows 58 to 63: Using yarn F.

Rows 64 to 67: Using yarn E.

Rows 68 to 72: Using yarn C.

Rows 73 to 78: Using yarn D.

Rows 79 to 83: Using yarn A.

Rows 84 to 91: Using yarn B.

Rows 92 to 98: Using yarn C.

Rows 99 to 102: Using yarn E.

Rows 103 to 107: Using yarn B.

Rows 108 to 111: Using yarn A.

Rows 112 to 114: Using yarn D.

Rows 115 to 118: Using yarn B.

Rows 119 to 124: Using yarn A.

Rows 125 to 127: Using yarn C.

Row 128: Using yarn E.

Rows 129 and 130: Using yarn B.

Rows 131 to 134: Using yarn D.

These 134 rows form stripe sequence A and should be repeated if required.

STRIPE SEQUENCE B

Beg with a K row and using all yarns DOUBLE, work in st st in stripes as folls:

Rows 1 to 6: Using yarn A.

Rows 7 to 9: Using yarn C.

Row 10: Using yarn E.

Rows 11 and 12: Using yarn B.

Row 13: Using yarn D.

Rows 14 to 18: Using yarn A.

Rows 19 and 20: Using yarn D.

Rows 21 to 27: Using yarn B.

Rows 28 to 30: Using yarn F.

Rows 31 to 36: Using yarn C.

Rows 37 to 41: Using yarn A.

Rows 42 to 46: Using yarn B.

Rows 47 to 53: Using yarn D.

Rows 54 to 57: Using yarn A.

Rows 58 to 63: Using yarn C.

Rows 64 to 71: Using yarn B.

Rows 72 to 77: Using yarn F.

Rows 78 to 81: Using yarn E.

Rows 82 to 86: Using yarn C.

Rows 87 to 92: Using yarn D.

ROWS 93 TO 97: Using yarn A.

Rows 98 to 100: Using yarn B.

These 100 rows form stripe sequence B and should be repeated if required.

BACK

Using 4mm (US 6) needles and yarn E DOUBLE, cast on 87 [87: 93: **99: 105: 105**] sts.

Row 1 (RS): K3, *P3, K3, rep from * to end.

Row 2: P3, *K3, P3, rep from * to end.

These 2 rows form rib.

Cont in rib using colours as folls:

Rows 3 to 6: Using yarn E.

Join in yarn F DOUBLE.

Rows 7 and 8: Using yarn F.

Rows 9 and 10: Using yarn E.

Rows 11 and 12: Using yarn F.

Rows 13 to 18: Using yarn E, dec [inc: -:
-: dec: inc] 1 st at each end of last row.
85 [89: 93: **99: 103: 107**] sts.

Change to 5mm (US 8) needles.

Remembering to use all yarns DOUBLE, now work in st st in stripe sequence A throughout (see above) and cont as folls:**

Work straight until back meas 40 cm, ending with RS facing for next row.

Shape armholes

Keeping stripes correct, cast off 4 sts at beg of next 2 rows. 77 [81: 85: **91: 95: 99**] sts.

Dec 1 st at each end of next 5 rows. 67 [71: 75: **81: 85: 89**] sts.

Cont straight until armhole meas 21 [22: 23: **24: 25: 26**] cm, ending with RS facing for next row.

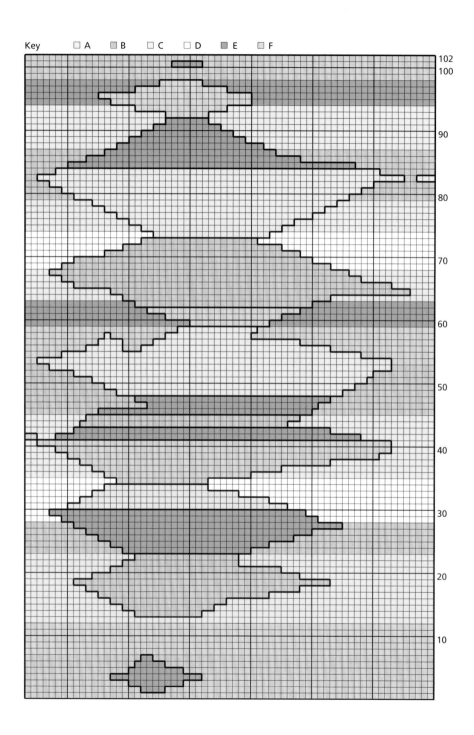

Key □ A ▨ B □ C □ D ▨ E ▨ F

Shape shoulders and back neck

Cast off 6 [7: 7: **8: 9: 9**] sts at beg of next 2 rows. 55 [57: 61: **65: 67: 71**] sts.

Next row (RS): Cast off 6 [7: 7: **8: 9: 9**] sts, K until there are 11 [11: 12: **12: 12: 13**] sts on right needle and turn, leaving rem sts on a holder.

Work each side of neck separately.

Cast off 4 sts at beg of next row.

Cast off rem 7 [7: 8: **8: 8: 9**] sts.

With RS facing, rejoin appropriate yarn to rem sts, cast off centre 21 [21: 23: **25: 25: 27**] sts, K to end.

Complete to match first side, reversing shapings.

FRONT

Work as given for back to **.

Work 4 rows, ending with RS facing for next row.

Place chart

Working edge sts in stripe sequence as now set, place chart as folls:

Row 1 (RS): K8 [10: 12: **15: 17: 19**], work next 67 sts as row 1 of chart, K to end.

Row 2: P10 [12: 14: **17: 19: 21**], work next

67 sts as row 2 of chart, P to end.

These 2 rows set position of chart.

Working rem 100 rows of chart and then completing front in stripe sequence across all sts, cont as folls:

Cont straight until front matches back to beg of armhole shaping, ending with RS facing for next row.

Shape armholes

Keeping stripes correct, cast off 4 sts at beg of next 2 rows. 77 [81: 85: **91: 95: 99**] sts.

Dec 1 st at each end of next 5 rows. 67 [71: 75: **81: 85: 89**] sts.

Cont straight until 12 [**14**] rows less have been worked than on back to beg of shoulder shaping, ending with RS facing for next row.

Shape neck

Next row (RS): K25 [27: 28: **31: 33: 34**] and turn, leaving rem sts on a holder.

Work each side of neck separately.

Dec 1 st at neck edge of next 4 rows, then on foll 1 [**2**] alt rows, then on foll 4th row. 19 [21: 22: **24: 26: 27**] sts.

Work 1 row, ending with RS facing for next row.

Shape shoulder

Cast off 6 [7: 7: **8: 9: 9**] sts at beg of next and foll alt row.

Work 1 row.

Cast off rem 7 [7: 8: **8: 8: 9**] sts.

With RS facing, rejoin appropriate yarn to rem sts, cast off centre 17 [17: 19: **19: 19: 21**] sts, K to end.

Complete to match first side, reversing shapings.

SLEEVES

Using 4mm (US 6) needles and yarn E DOUBLE, cast on 39 [39: 45: **45: 45: 51**] sts.

Work in rib as given for back using colours as folls:

Rows 1 to 6: Using yarn E.

Join in yarn F DOUBLE.

Rows 7 and 8: Using yarn F.

Rows 9 and 10: Using yarn E.

Rows 11 and 12: Using yarn F.

Rows 13 to 18: Using yarn E, - [inc: dec: -: inc: dec] 1 st at each end of last row. 39 [41: 43: **45: 47: 49**] sts.

Change to 5mm (US 8) needles.

Remembering to use all yarns DOUBLE, now work in st st in stripe sequence B throughout (see above) and cont as folls:

Inc 1 st at each end of 5th and every foll 6th [**6th: 6th: 4th**] row to 47 [**51: 51: 89**] sts, then on every foll 4th [**4th: 4th: -**] row until there are 71 [75: 79: **81: 85: -**] sts.

Cont straight until sleeve meas 45 [46: 47: **48: 49: 50**] cm, ending with RS facing for next row.

Shape top

Keeping stripes correct, cast off 4 sts at beg of next 2 rows. 63 [67: 71: **73: 77: 81**] sts.

Dec 1 st at each end of next and foll 3 alt rows, then on foll row, ending with RS facing for next row.

Cast off rem 53 [57: 61: **63: 67: 71**] sts.

MAKING UP

Press as described on the information page. Join right shoulder seam using back stitch, or mattress stitch if preferred.

Neckband

With RS facing, using 4mm (US 6) needles and yarn E DOUBLE, pick up and knit 14 [14: 15: **17: 17: 18**] sts down left side of neck, 17 [17: 19: **19: 19: 21**] sts from front, 14 [14: 15: **17: 17: 18**] sts up right side of neck, then 30 [30: 32: **34: 34: 36**] sts from back. 75 [75: 81: **87: 87: 93**] sts.

Beg with row 2, work in rib as given for back using colours as folls:

Rows 1 to 5: Using yarn E.

Rows 6 and 7: Using yarn F.

Rows 8 and 9: Using yarn E.

Rows 10 and 11: Using yarn F.

Rows 12 to 15: Using yarn E.

Row 16 (RS): Using yarn F.

Cast off in rib using yarn F (on WS).

See information page for finishing instructions, setting in sleeves using the shallow set-in method.

SASSY BOLERO
Jean Moss

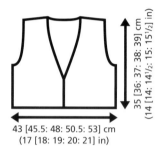

35 [36: 37: 38: 39] cm
(14 [14: 14½: 15: 15½] in)

43 [45.5: 48: 50.5: 53] cm
(17 [18: 19: 20: 21] in)

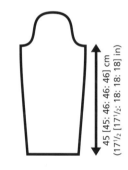

45 [45: 46: 46: 46] cm
(17½ [17½: 18: 18: 18] in)

SIZES & YARNS

XS	S	M	L	XL	

To fit bust

81	86	91	97	102	cm
32	34	36	38	40	in

Rowan Scottish Tweed Aran

4	4	4	5	5	x 100gm

(photographed in Porridge 024)

NEEDLES

1 pair 4mm (no 8) (US 6) needles
1 pair 5mm (no 6) (US 8) needles
4mm (no 8) (US 6) circular needle

TENSION

16 sts and 23 rows to 10 cm measured over
stocking stitch using 5mm (US 8) needles.

SPECIAL ABBREVIATION

MK = make knot as folls: (K1, P1, K1, P1,
K1) all into next st, lift 2nd, 3rd, 4th and
5th sts on right needle over first st and
off needle.

BACK

Using 4mm (US 6) needles, cast on 69 [73: 77: 81: 85] sts.

Beg rib as folls:

Row 1 (RS): K1, *P1, K1, rep from * to end.

Row 2: P1, *K1, P1, rep from * to end.

These 2 rows form rib.

Work in rib for a further 2 rows, ending with RS facing for next row.

Change to 5mm (US 8) needles.

Place charts

Next row (RS): K8 [10: 12: 13: 15], work next 15 sts as row 1 of chart, K23 [23: 23: 25: 25], work next 15 sts as row 1 of chart, K8 [10: 12: 13: 15].

Next row: P8 [10: 12: 13: 15], work next 15 sts as row 2 of chart, P23 [23: 23: 25: 25], work next 15 sts as row 2 of chart, P8 [10: 12: 13: 15].

These 2 rows set the sts – 2 charts with st st between and at sides.

Cont as set until back meas 16 [17: 17: 18: 18] cm, ending with RS facing for next row.

Shape armholes

Keeping patt correct, cast off 4 sts at beg of next 2 rows. 61 [65: 69: 73: 77] sts.

Dec 1 st at each end of next 3 [3: 5: 5: 7] rows, then on foll 0 [1: 1: 2: 2] alt rows. 55 [57: 57: 59: 59] sts.

Cont straight until armhole meas 19 [19: 20: 20: 21] cm, ending with RS facing for next row.

Shape shoulders and back neck

Cast off 9 sts at beg of next 2 rows, then 9 [10: 10: 10: 10] sts at beg of foll 2 rows.

Cast off rem 19 [19: 19: 21: 21] sts.

LEFT FRONT

Using 4mm (US 6) needles, cast on 34 [36: 38: 40: 42] sts.

Row 1 (RS): *K1, P1, rep from * to end.

Row 2: As row 1.

These 2 rows form rib.

Work in rib for a further 2 rows, ending with RS facing for next row.

Change to 5mm (US 8) needles.

Place chart

Next row (RS): K8 [10: 12: 13: 15], work next 15 sts as row 1 of chart, K11 [11: 11: 12: 12].

Next row: P11 [11: 11: 12: 12], work next 15 sts as row 2 of chart, P8 [10: 12: 13: 15].

These 2 rows set the sts – chart on page 72 with st st at sides.

Cont as set until 20 rows less have been worked than on back to beg of armhole shaping, ending with RS facing for next row.

Shape front slope

Keeping patt correct, dec 1 st at end of next and every foll 6th row until 30 [32: 34: 36: 38] sts rem.

Work 1 row, ending with RS facing for next row. (Left front should now match back to beg of armhole shaping.)

Shape armhole

Keeping patt correct, cast off 4 sts at beg of next row. 26 [28: 30: 32: 34] sts.

Work 1 row.

Dec 1 st at armhole edge of next 3 [3: 5: 5: 7] rows, then on foll 0 [1: 1: 2: 2] alt rows and at same time dec 1 st at front slope edge on 3rd [3rd: 5th: 3rd: 3rd] and foll 0 [0: 0: 6th: 6th] row. 22 [23: 23: 23: 23] sts.

Dec 1 st at front slope edge only on 8th [6th: 6th: 6th: 4th] and every foll 8th [8th: 8th: 6th: 8th] row to 18 [19: 19: 21: 19] sts, then on every foll – [-: -: 8th: -] row until – [-: -: 19: -] sts rem.

Cont straight until left front matches back to beg of shoulder shaping, ending with RS facing for next row.

Shape shoulder

Cast off 9 sts at beg of next row.

Work 1 row.

Cast off rem 9 [10: 10: 10: 10] sts.

RIGHT FRONT

Using 4mm (US 6) needles, cast on 34 [36: 38: 40: 42] sts.

Beg rib as folls:

Row 1 (RS): *P1, K1, rep from * to end.

Row 2: As row 1.

These 2 rows form rib.

Work in rib for a further 2 rows, ending with RS facing for next row.

Change to 5mm (US 8) needles.

Place chart

Next row (RS): K11 [11: 11: 12: 12], work next 15 sts as row 1 of chart, K8 [10: 12: 13: 15].

Next row: P8 [10: 12: 13: 15], work next 15 sts as row 2 of chart, P11 [11: 11: 12: 12].

These 2 rows set the sts – chart with st st at sides.

32 row patt repeat

Key

☐ K on RS,
P on WS

◙ yfwd

☑ K2tog

◩ sl1, K1, psso

▨ sl1, K2tog, psso

▣ MK

Complete to match left front, reversing shapings.

SLEEVES

Using 4mm (US 6) needles, cast on 33 [33: 35: 37: 37] sts.

Work in rib as given for back for 6 rows, ending with RS facing for next row.

Change to 5mm (US 8) needles.

Work in rib for a further 14 rows, inc 1 st at each end of 7th [7th: 7th: 9th: 7th] of these rows and ending with RS facing for next row. 35 [35: 37: 39: 39] sts.

Place chart

Next row (RS): K10 [10: 11: 12: 12], work next 15 sts as row 1 of chart, K10 [10: 11: 12: 12].

Next row: P10 [10: 11: 12: 12], work next 15 sts as row 2 of chart, P10 [10: 11: 12: 12].

These 2 rows set the sts – chart with st st at sides.

Cont as set, shaping sides by inc 1 st at each end of 3rd [3rd: 3rd: 9th: 3rd] and every foll 12th [12th: 14th: 16th: 14th] row to 39 [39: 49: 49: 51] sts, then on every foll 14th [14th:

-: -: -] row until there are 47 [47: -: -: -] sts, taking inc sts into st st.

Cont straight until sleeve meas 45 [45: 46: 46: 46] cm, ending with RS facing for next row.

Shape top

Keeping patt correct, cast off 4 sts at beg of next 2 rows. 39 [39: 41: 41: 43] sts.

Dec 1 st at each end of next and foll 3 alt rows, then on every foll 4th row to 23 [23: 25: 25: 27] sts, then on every foll alt row until 17 sts rem.

Work 1 row, ending with RS facing for next row.

Cast off rem 17 sts.

MAKING UP

Press as described on the information page. Join both shoulder seams using back stitch, or mattress stitch if preferred.

Front border

With RS facing and using 4mm (US 6) circular needle, beg and ending at cast-on edges, pick up and knit 12 [13: 13: 15: 15] sts up right front opening edge to beg of front slope shaping, 45 [45: 46: 46: 48] sts

up right front slope to shoulder, 19 [19: 19: 21: 21] sts from back, 45 [45: 46: 46: 48] sts down left front slope to beg of front slope shaping, then 12 [13: 13: 15: 15] sts down left front opening edge. 133 [135: 137: 143: 147] sts.

Next row (WS): Knit.

Work picot cast-off as folls: cast off 2 sts (one st on right needle), *slip st on right needle back onto left needle, cast on 2 sts, cast off 4 sts (one st on right needle), rep from * to end.

Fasten off.

See information page for finishing instructions, setting in sleeves using the set-in method.

SCOTTIE DOG JACKET
Sasha Kagan

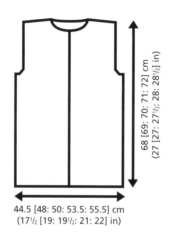

68 [69: 70: 71: 72] cm
(27 [27: 27½: 28: 28½] in)

44.5 [48: 50: 53.5: 55.5] cm
(17½ [19: 19½: 21: 22] in)

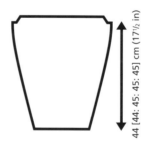

44 [44: 45: 45: 45] cm (17½ in)

SIZES & YARNS

	XS	S	M	L	XL	
To fit bust						
	81	86	91	97	102	cm
	32	34	36	38	40	in

Rowan Scottish Tweed Aran

	XS	S	M	L	XL	
A Porridge 024	1	1	1	1	2	x 100gm
B Thistle 016	1	1	1	1	1	x 100gm
C Thatch 018	1	1	1	1	1	x 100gm
D Lewis Grey 007	2	2	2	3	3	x 100gm
E Midnight 023	5	5	5	6	6	x 100gm
F Lavender 005	2	2	3	3	3	x 100gm

NEEDLES

1 pair 4mm (no 8) (US 6) needles
1 pair 5mm (no 6) (US 8) needles

BUTTONS

3 x Rowan No. 00343

TENSION

18 sts and 23 rows to 10 cm measured over patterned stocking stitch, 16 sts and 27 rows to 10 cm measured over moss stitch, both using 5mm (US 8) needles.

BACK

Using 4mm (US 6) needles and yarn E, cast on 79 [85: 89: 95: 99] sts.
Row 1 (RS): K1, *P1, K1, rep from * to end.
Row 2: As row 1.
These 2 rows form moss st.
Work in moss st for a further 4 rows, inc 1 st at end of last row and ending with RS facing for next row. 80 [86: 90: 96: 100] sts.
Change to 5mm (US 8) needles.
Beg and ending rows as indicated, using the intarsia technique as described on the information page and repeating the 44 row

patt repeat throughout, cont in patt from chart, which is worked entirely in st st beg with a K row, as folls:
Cont in patt until back meas 46 [47: 47: 48: 48] cm, ending with RS facing for next row.
Shape armholes
Keeping patt correct, cast off 5 sts at beg of next 2 rows. 70 [76: 80: 86: 90] sts.
Dec 1 st at each end of next 5 rows. 60 [66: 70: 76: 80] sts.
Cont straight until armhole meas 22 [22: 23: 23: 24] cm, ending with RS facing for next row.
Shape shoulders and back neck
Cast off 5 [6: 7: 7: 8] sts at beg of next 2 rows. 50 [54: 56: 62: 64] sts.
Next row (RS): Cast off 5 [6: 7: 7: 8] sts, patt until there are 10 [10: 10: 12: 12] sts on right needle and turn, leaving rem sts on a holder.
Work each side of neck separately.
Cast off 4 sts at beg of next row.
Cast off rem 6 [6: 6: 8: 8] sts.
With RS facing, rejoin yarns to rem sts, cast off centre 20 [22: 22: 24: 24] sts, patt to end.
Complete to match first side, reversing shapings.

POCKET LININGS (make 2)

Using 5mm (US 8) needles and yarn E, cast on 22 sts.
Beg with a K row, work in st st for 36 rows, ending with RS facing for next row.
Break yarn and leave sts on a holder.

LEFT FRONT

Using 4mm (US 6) needles and yarn E, cast on 45 [47: 49: 53: 55] sts.
Work in moss st as given for back for 5 rows, ending with WS facing for next row.
Row 6 (WS): Moss st 5 sts and slip these 5 sts onto a holder, moss st to last 0 [1: 1: 0: 0] st, (inc in last st) 0 [1: 1: 0: 0] times. 40 [43: 45: 48: 50] sts.
Change to 5mm (US 8) needles.
Beg and ending rows as indicated, cont in patt from chart as folls:
Work 44 rows, ending with RS facing for next row.
Place pocket
Next row (RS): Patt 8 [9: 10: 11: 12] sts, slip next 22 sts onto a holder and, in their place, patt across 22 sts of first pocket lining, patt to end.

Cont straight until left front matches back to beg of armhole shaping, ending with RS facing for next row.
Shape armhole
Keeping patt correct, cast off 5 sts at beg of next row. 35 [38: 40: 43: 45] sts.
Work 1 row.
Dec 1 st at armhole edge of next 5 rows. 30 [33: 35: 38: 40] sts.
Cont straight until 13 [13: 13: 15: 15] rows less have been worked than on back to beg of shoulder shaping, ending with WS facing for next row.
Shape neck
Keeping patt correct, cast off 6 [7: 7: 7: 7] sts at beg of next row, then 3 sts at beg of foll alt row. 21 [23: 25: 28: 30] sts.
Dec 1 st at neck edge of next 3 rows, then on foll 1 [1: 1: 2: 2] alt rows, then on foll 4th row. 16 [18: 20: 22: 24] sts.
Work 1 row, ending with RS facing for next row.
Shape shoulder
Cast off 5 [6: 7: 7: 8] sts at beg of next and foll alt row.
Work 1 row. Cast off rem 6 [6: 6: 8: 8] sts.

RIGHT FRONT

Using 4mm (US 6) needles and yarn E, cast on 45 [47: 49: 53: 55] sts.

Work in moss st as given for back for 5 rows, ending with WS facing for next row.

Row 6 (WS): (Inc in first st) 0 [1: 1: 0: 0] times, moss st to last 5 sts and turn, leaving last 5 sts on a holder. 40 [43: 45: 48: 50] sts.

Change to 5mm (US 8) needles.

Beg and ending rows as indicated, cont in patt from chart as folls:

Work 44 rows, ending with RS facing for next row.

Place pocket

Next row (RS): Patt 10 [12: 13: 15: 16] sts, slip next 22 sts onto a holder and, in their place, patt across 22 sts of second pocket lining, patt to end.

Complete to match left front, reversing shapings.

SLEEVES

Using 4mm (US 6) needles and yarn E, cast on 37 [37: 39: 41: 41] sts.

Work in moss st as given for back for 8 rows, ending with RS facing for next row.

Change to 5mm (US 8) needles.

Cont in moss st, shaping sides by inc 1 st at each end of next and every foll 8th [8th: 8th: 8th: 6th] row to 47 [47: 45: 53: 75] sts, then on every foll 6th [6th: 6th: 6th: 4th] row until there are 69 [69: 73: 73: 77] sts.

Cont straight until sleeve meas 44 [44: 45: 45: 45] cm, ending with RS facing for next row.

Shape top

Cast off 5 sts at beg of next 2 rows. 59 [59: 63: 63: 67] sts.

Dec 1 st at each end of next and foll 3 alt rows, then on foll row, ending with RS facing for next row.

Cast off rem 49 [49: 53: 53: 57] sts.

MAKING UP

Press as described on the information page.

Join both shoulder seams using back stitch, or mattress stitch if preferred.

Left front border

Slip 5 sts from left front holder onto 4mm (US 6) needles and rejoin yarn E with RS facing.

Cont in moss st as set until border, when slightly stretched, fits up left front opening edge to neck shaping, ending with RS facing for next row.

Break yarn and leave sts on a holder.

Right front border

Slip 5 sts from right front holder onto 4mm (US 6) needles and rejoin yarn E with WS facing.

Cont in moss st as set until border, when slightly stretched, fits up right front opening edge to neck shaping, ending with RS facing for next row.

Do NOT break yarn.

Slip stitch borders in place.

Hood

With RS facing, using 4mm (US 6) needles and ball of yarn E attached to right front border, moss st 5 sts of right front border, pick up and knit 22 [23: 23: 25: 25] sts up right side of neck, 29 [31: 31: 33: 33] sts from back, 22 [23: 23: 25: 25] sts down left side of neck, then moss st 5 sts of left front border. 83 [87: 87: 93: 93] sts.

Change to 5mm (US 8) needles.

Keeping moss st correct throughout as set by front border sts, work in moss st under hood

meas 29 [30: 30: 31: 31] cm, ending with RS facing for next row.

Cast off 27 [29: 29: 31: 31] sts at beg of next 2 rows. 29 [29: 29: 31: 31] sts.

Cont straight until hood meas 17 [18: 18: 19: 19] cm from cast-off sts, ending with RS facing for next row.

Cast off.

Join hood seams by joining row-end edges of last section to cast-off sts.

Pocket tops (both alike)

Slip 22 sts from pocket holder onto 4mm (US 6) needles and rejoin yarn E with RS facing.

Row 1 (RS): K10, K2tog, K10. 21 sts.

Work in moss st as given for back for 4 rows, ending with WS facing for next row.

Cast off in moss st (on WS).

See information page for finishing instructions, setting in sleeves using the shallow set-in method.

Using yarn E, make 3 crochet or twisted cords, each 8 cm long, and attach to right front border to form button loops.

Key ☐ A ■ B ▨ C ▨ D ▣ E ☐ F

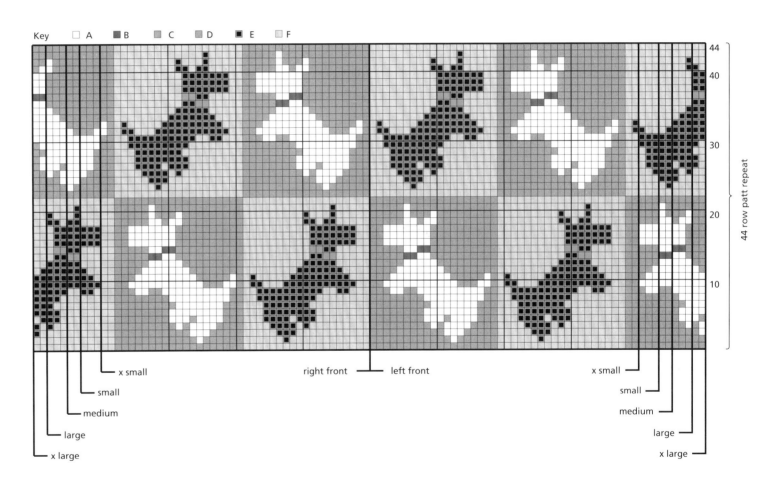

44 row patt repeat

x small

small

medium

large

x large

right front — left front

x small

small

medium

large

x large

SUGARBABE CARDIGAN
Jean Moss

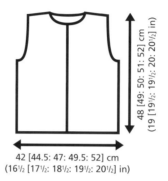

48 [49: 50: 51: 52] cm
(19 [19½: 19½: 20: 20½] in)

42 [44.5: 47: 49.5: 52] cm
(16½ [17½: 18½: 19½: 20½] in)

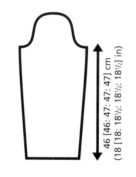

46 [46: 47: 47: 47] cm
(18 [18: 18½: 18½: 18½] in)

SIZES & YARNS

	XS	S	M	L	XL	
To fit bust						
	81	86	91	97	102	cm
	32	34	36	38	40	in

Rowan Scottish Tweed DK

		XS	S	M	L	XL	
A	Thistle 016						
		7	8	8	8	9	x 50gm
B	Lavender 005						
		3	3	3	3	4	x 50gm
C	Herring 008						
		1	1	1	1	1	x 50gm
D	Skye 003						
		1	1	1	1	1	x 50gm
E	Apple 015						
		1	1	1	1	1	x 50gm
F	Thatch 018						
		1	1	1	1	1	x 50gm

NEEDLES

1 pair 3¼mm (no 10) (US 3) needles
1 pair 4mm (no 8) (US 6) needles

BUTTONS

8 x Rowan No. 00324

TENSION

24 sts and 26 rows to 10 cm measured over patterned stocking stitch, 24 sts and 24 rows to 10 cm measured over fancy rib, both using 4mm (US 6) needles.

SPECIAL ABBREVIATION

Tw2 = K2tog tbl leaving sts on left needle, K tog same 2 sts again and slip both sts off left needle.

BACK

Using 3¼mm (US 3) needles and yarn A, cast on 102 [106: 114: 118: 126] sts.
Row 1 (WS): K2, *P2, K2, rep from * to end.
Row 2: P2, *Tw2, P2, rep from * to end.
Row 3: K2, *P1, yrn, P1, K2, rep from * to end.
Row 4: P2, *sl 1, K1, psso, K1, P2, rep from * to end.
These 4 rows form fancy rib.
Work in fancy rib for a further 48 rows, ending with WS facing for next row.
Change to 4mm (US 6) needles.
Purl 1 row, dec [inc: dec: inc: dec] 1 st at end of row and ending with RS facing for next row. 101 [107: 113: 119: 125] sts.
Beg and ending rows as indicated, using the Fair Isle technique as described on the information page and repeating the 26 row patt repeat throughout, cont in patt from chart for body, which is worked entirely in st st beg with a K row, as folls:
Cont in patt until back meas 29 [30: 30: 31: 31] cm, ending with RS facing for next row.
Shape armholes
Keeping patt correct, cast off 4 [5: 5: 6: 6] sts at beg of next 2 rows. 93 [97: 103: 107: 113] sts.
Dec 1 st at each end of next 5 [6: 8: 9: 11] rows. 83 [85: 87: 89: 91] sts.
Cont straight until armhole meas 19 [19: 20: 20: 21] cm, ending with RS facing for next row.
Shape shoulders and back neck
Cast off 9 [9: 9: 9: 10] sts at beg of next 2 rows. 65 [67: 69: 71: 71] sts.
Next row (RS): Cast off 9 [9: 9: 9: 10] sts, patt until there are 13 [13: 14: 14: 13] sts on right needle and turn, leaving rem sts on a holder.
Work each side of neck separately.
Cast off 4 sts at beg of next row.
Cast off rem 9 [9: 10: 10: 9] sts.
With RS facing, rejoin yarns to rem sts, cast off centre 21 [23: 23: 25: 25] sts, patt to end.
Complete to match first side, reversing shapings.

LEFT FRONT

Using 3¼mm (US 3) needles and yarn A, cast on 54 [58: 62: 66: 66] sts.
Work in fancy rib as given for back for 52 rows, ending with WS facing for next row.
Change to 4mm (US 6) needles.
Row 53 (WS): Rib 6 sts and slip these 6 sts onto a holder, (P28, P2tog) 0 [0: 0: 1: 0] times, P to last 1 [0: 2: 2: 1] sts, (inc in last st) 1 [0: 0: 0: 1] times, (P2tog) 0 [0: 1: 1: 0] times. 49 [52: 55: 58: 61] sts.
Beg and ending rows as indicated, cont in patt from chart for body as folls:
Cont in patt until left front matches back to beg of armhole shaping, ending with RS facing for next row.
Shape armhole
Keeping patt correct, cast off 4 [5: 5: 6: 6] sts at beg of next row. 45 [47: 50: 52: 55] sts.
Work 1 row.
Dec 1 st at armhole edge of next 5 [6: 8: 9: 11] rows. 40 [41: 42: 43: 44] sts.
Cont straight until 13 [13: 13: 15: 15] rows less have been worked than on back to beg of shoulder shaping, ending with WS facing for next row.
Shape neck
Keeping patt correct, cast off 5 [6: 6: 6: 6] sts at beg of next row. 35 [35: 36: 37: 38] sts.
Dec 1 st at neck edge of next 5 rows, then

Sleeve chart

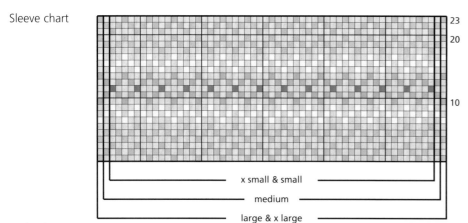

x small & small

medium

large & x large

23
20

10

Body chart

Key ■ A ☐ B ▨ C ☐ D ▨ E ▨ F

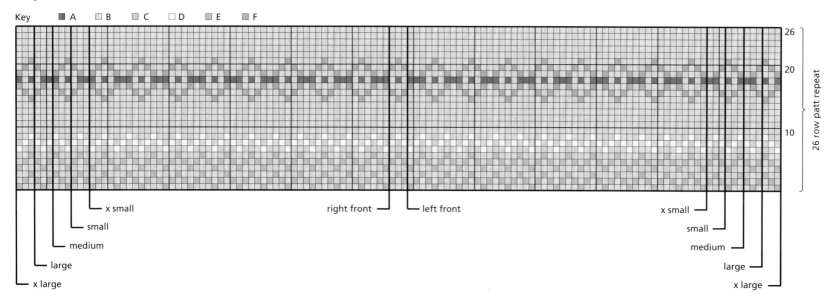

x small

small

medium

large

x large

right front

left front

x small

small

medium

large

x large

26

20

10

26 row patt repeat

on foll 3 [3: 3: 4: 4] alt rows. 27 [27: 28: 28: 29] sts.

Work 1 row, ending with RS facing for next row.

Shape shoulder

Cast off 9 [9: 9: 9: 10] sts at beg of next and foll alt row.

Work 1 row.

Cast off rem 9 [9: 10: 10: 9] sts.

RIGHT FRONT

Using 3¼mm (US 3) needles and yarn A, cast on 54 [58: 62: 66: 66] sts.

Work in fancy rib as given for back for 52 rows, ending with WS facing for next row.

Change to 4mm (US 6) needles.

Row 53 (WS): (Inc in first st) 1 [0: 0: 0: 1] times, (P2tog) 0 [0: 1: 1: 0] times, (P28, P2tog) 0 [0: 0: 1: 0] times, P to last 6 sts and turn, leaving rem 6 sts on a holder. 49 [52: 55: 58: 61] sts.

Beg and ending rows as indicated, cont in patt from chart for body and complete to match left front, reversing shapings.

SLEEVES

Using 3¼mm (US 3) needles and yarn A, cast on 54 [54: 54: 58: 58] sts.

Work in fancy rib as given for back for 24 rows, dec [dec: inc: dec: dec] 1 st at end of last row and ending with WS facing for next row. 53 [53: 55: 57: 57] sts.

Row 26 (WS): Knit (to form fold line).

Change to 4mm (US 6) needles.

Beg and ending rows as indicated, cont in patt from chart for cuff as folls:

Work 23 rows, ending with WS facing for next row.

Break off contrasts and cont using yarn A only.

Next row (WS): P4 [4: 9: 2: 2], inc in next st, (P10 [10: 17: 12: 12], inc in next st) 4 [4: 2: 4: 4] times, P to end. 58 [58: 58: 62: 62] sts.

Beg with row 2, cont in fancy rib patt as given for back, shaping sides by inc 1 st at

each end of 13th [11th: 9th: 11th: 9th] and every foll 14th [12th: 10th: 12th: 10th] row to 62 [66: 62: 66: 66] sts, then on every foll 16th [14th: 12th: 14th: 12th] row until there are 68 [70: 72: 74: 76] sts, taking inc sts into patt.

Cont straight until sleeve meas 46 [46: 47: 47: 47] cm from fold line row, ending with RS facing for next row.

Shape top

Keeping patt correct, cast off 4 [5: 5: 6: 6] sts at beg of next 2 rows. 60 [60: 62: 62: 64] sts.

Dec 1 st at each end of next and every foll alt row to 34 sts, then on foll 3 rows, ending with RS facing for next row. 28 sts.

Cast off 3 sts at beg of next 4 rows.

Cast off rem 16 sts.

MAKING UP

Press as described on the information page. Join both shoulder seams using back stitch, or mattress stitch if preferred.

Left front band

Slip 6 sts from left front holder onto 3¼mm (US 3) needles and rejoin yarn A with RS facing.

Cont in fancy rib as set until band, when slightly stretched, fits up left front opening edge to neck shaping, ending with RS facing for next row.

Cast off.

Right front band

Slip 6 sts from right front holder onto 3¼mm (US 3) needles and rejoin yarn A with WS facing.

Cont in fancy rib as set until band, when slightly stretched, fits up right front opening edge to neck shaping, ending with RS facing for next row.

Cast off. Slip stitch borders in place.

Collar

With RS facing, using 3¼mm (US 3) needles and yarn A, beg and ending half way across top of bands, pick up and knit 36 [37: 37: 38: 38] sts up right side of neck, 30 [32: 32: 34: 34] sts from back, then 36 [37: 37: 38: 38] sts down left side of neck. 102 [106: 106: 110: 110] sts.

Row 1 (RS of collar, WS of body): K2, P2, *Tw2, P2, rep from * to last 2 sts, K2.

Row 2: P2, K2, *P1, yrn, P1, K2, rep from * to last 2 sts, P2.

Row 3: K2, P2, *sl 1, K1, psso, K1, P2, rep from * to last 2 sts, K2.

Row 4: P2, *K2, P2, rep from * to end.

These 4 rows form fancy rib.

Change to 4mm (US 6) needles.

Cont in fancy rib patt until collar meas 8 cm, ending with RS facing for next row.

Cast off in patt.

See information page for finishing instructions, setting in sleeves using the set-in method. Fold first 24 rows of sleeves to inside along fold line row and slip stitch in place. Attach 8 buttons to left front band, placing buttons approx 2 cm from ends of band and using "yrn" of patt row 3 as buttonholes.

MONDRIAN-STYLE BLANKET
Di Gilpin

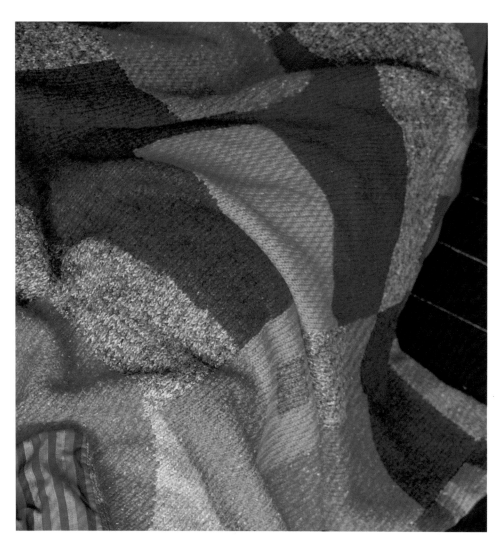

SIZE & YARNS

**Rowan ScottishTweed 4 ply, DK and Aran

A Aran Thatch 018
1 x 100gm

B Aran Rust 009
2 x 100gm

C Aran Claret 013
2 x 100gm

D Aran Thistle 016
2 x 100gm

E DK Apple 015
1 x 50gm

F 4 ply Apple 015
1 x 25gm

G Aran Lavender 005
2 x 100gm

H DK Sunset 011
3 x 50gm

J 4 ply Rust 009
4 x 25gm

L DK Lobster 017
4 x 50gm

M 4 ply Wine 012
4 x 25gm

N DK Lewis Grey 007
5 x 50gm

Q 4 ply Storm Grey 004
5 x 25gm

R Aran Brill Pink 010
1 x 100gm

S DK Sunset 011
1 x 50gm

T 4 ply Sunset 011
1 x 25gm

**DK and 4 ply worked together at all times

NEEDLES

1 pair 5mm (no 6) (US 8) needles

EXTRAS

Piece of backing fabric 190 cm (75 in) x 140 cm (55 in)

FINISHED SIZE

Completed blanket measures 135 cm (53 in) by 182 cm (71½ in).

TENSION

16 sts and 23 rows to 10 cm measured over stocking stitch using 5mm (US 8) needles.

RIGHT PANEL

Using 5mm (US 8) needles and yarns L and M held together, cast on 53 sts.

Beg with a K row, work in st st for 40 rows, ending with RS facing for next row.

Break off yarns L and M and join in yarns N and Q held together.

Work 10 rows, ending with RS facing for next row.

Using the intarsia technique as described on the information page, work 70 rows in patt from chart A, which is worked entirely in st st beg with a K row, ending with RS facing for next row.

Using yarns N and Q held together, work 60 rows.

Break off yarns N and Q and join in yarn G. Work 70 rows, ending with RS facing for next row. Break off yarn G.

Using the intarsia technique as described on the information page and joining in and breaking off yarns as required, cont as folls:

Row 251 (RS): Using yarn B K32, using yarn A K21.

Row 252: Using yarn A P21, using yarn B P32.

Rep last 2 rows 14 times more.

Row 281 (RS): Using yarn B K32, using yarns H and S held together K21.

Row 282: Using yarns H and S held together P21, using yarn B P32.

Rep last 2 rows 19 times more.

Row 321 (RS): Using yarns H and J held together K32, using yarns H and S held together K21.

Row 322: Using yarns H and S held together P21, using yarns H and J held together P32.

Rep last 2 rows 9 times more.

Row 341 (RS): Using yarns H and J held together K32, using yarns N and Q held together K21.

Row 342: Using yarns N and Q held together P21, using yarns H and J held together P32.

Rep last 2 rows 19 times more.

Cast off.

CENTRE PANEL

Using 5mm (US 8) needles and yarns N and Q held together, cast on 87 sts.

Beg with a K row, work in st st for 40 rows, ending with RS facing for next row.

Break off yarns N and Q and join in yarn C.

Work 10 rows, ending with RS facing for next row.

Using the intarsia technique as described on the information page, work 210 rows in patt from chart B, which is worked entirely in st st beg with a K row, ending with RS facing for next row.

Using the intarsia technique as described on the information page and joining in and breaking off yarns as required, cont as folls:

Row 261 (RS): Using yarns L and M held together K27, using yarns N and Q held together K24, using yarn C K16, using yarn R K20.

Row 262: Using yarn R P20, using yarn C P16, using yarns N and Q held together P24, using yarns L and M held together P27.

Rep last 2 rows 9 times more.

Row 281 (RS): Using yarns H and S held together K19, using yarn B K48, using yarn R K20.

Row 282: Using yarn R P20, using yarn B P48, using yarns H and S held together P19.

Rep last 2 rows 4 times more.

Row 291 (RS): Using yarns H and S held together K19, using yarn B K48, using yarns

H and S held together K20.

Row 292: Using yarns H and S held together P20, using yarn B P48, using yarns H and S held together P19.

Rep last 2 rows 8 times more.

Row 309 (RS): Using yarns H and S held together K19, using yarn D K24, using yarn C K44.

Row 310: Using yarn C P44, using yarn D P24, using yarns H and S held together P19.

Rep last 2 rows 15 times more.

Row 341 (RS): Using yarns N and Q held together K19, using yarn D K24, using yarn C K44.

Row 342: Using yarn C P44, using yarn D P24, using yarns N and Q held together P19.

Rep last 2 rows once more.

Row 345 (RS): Using yarns N and Q held together K19, using yarn A K24, using yarn C K44.

Row 346: Using yarn C P44, using yarn A P24, using yarns N and Q held together P19.

Rep last 2 rows twice more.

Row 351 (RS): Using yarns N and Q held together K19, using yarn G K24, using yarn C K44.

Key

A

B

C

D

G

H & J held together

L & M held together

N & Q held together

R

Chart A

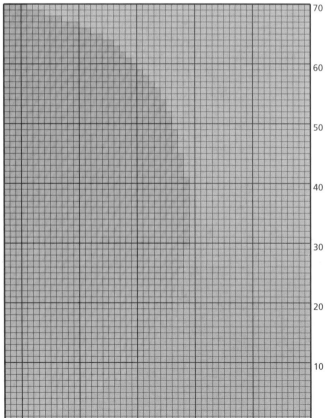

Chart B

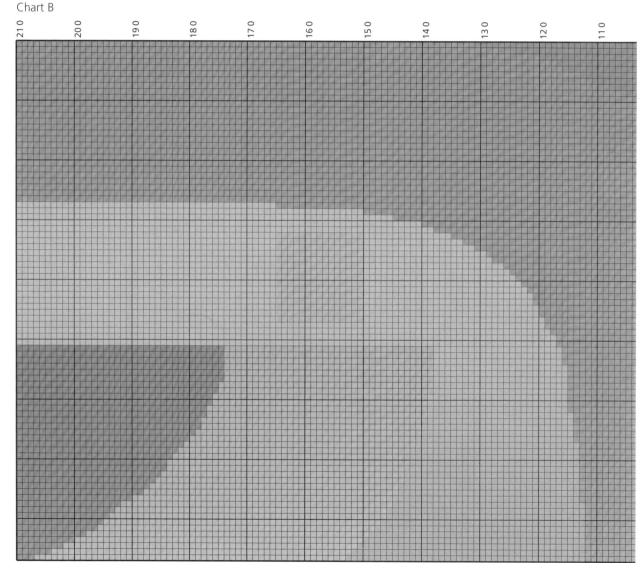

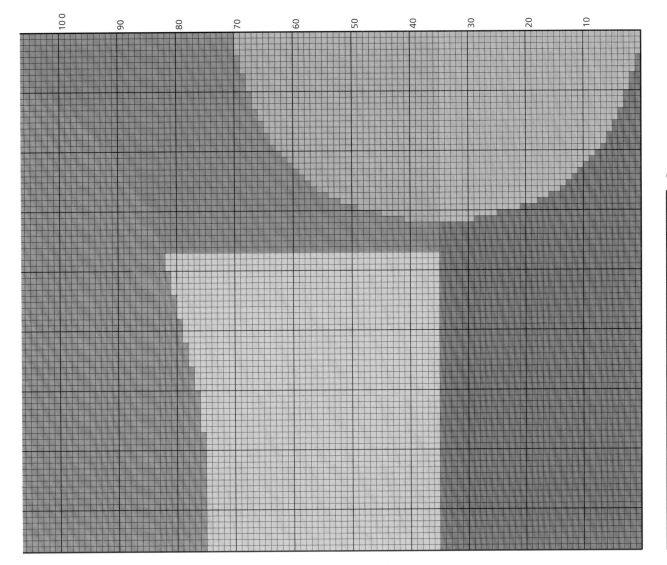

Chart C

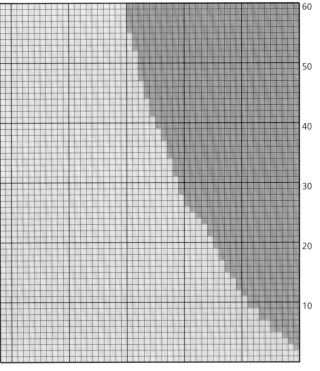

Row 352: Using yarn C P44, using yarn G P24, using yarns N and Q held together P19.
Rep last 2 rows 14 times more.
Cast off.

LEFT PANEL

Using 5mm (US 8) needles and yarn D, cast on 52 sts.
Beg with a K row, work in st st for 40 rows, ending with RS facing for next row.
Using the intarsia technique as described on the information page (see page 96) and joining in and breaking off yarns as required, cont as folls:

Row 41 (RS): Using yarn A K20, using yarns H and J held together K32.
Row 42: Using yarns H and J held together P32, using yarn A P20.
Rep last 2 rows 14 times more.
Row 71 (RS): Using yarns N and Q held together K20, using yarns H and J held together K32.
Row 72: Using yarns H and J held together P32, using yarns N and Q held together P20.
Rep last 2 rows 26 times more.
Row 125: As row 71.

Row 126 (WS): Using yarns H and S held together P22, using yarn R P30.
Row 127: Using yarn R K30, using yarns H and S held together K22.
Rep last 2 rows 5 times more.
Row 138: As row 126.
Row 139: Using yarn R K10, using yarn A K10, using yarn R K10, using yarns H and S held together P22.
Row 140: Using yarns H and S held together P22, using yarn R P10, using yarn A P10, using yarn R P10.
Rep last 2 rows 5 times more.
Row 151: As row 127.
Row 152: As row 126.
Rep last 2 rows 5 times more.
Using yarn B, work 38 rows, ending with RS facing for next row.
Using the intarsia technique as described on the information page, work 60 rows in patt from chart C, which is worked entirely in st st beg with a K row, ending with RS facing for next row.
Using the intarsia technique as described on the information page and joining in and breaking off yarns as required, cont as folls:

Row 261 (RS): Using yarns H and J held together K30, using yarn G K22.
Row 262: Using yarn G P22, using yarns H and J held together P30.
Rep last 2 rows 7 times more.
Row 277: As row 261.
Row 278 (WS): Using yarns N and Q held together P22, using yarns H and J held together P30.
Row 279: Using yarns H and J held together K30, using yarns N and Q held together K22.
Rep last 2 rows 14 times more.
Row 308: As row 278.
Row 309 (RS): Using yarn A K20, using yarns L and M held together K32.
Row 310: Using yarns L and M held together P32, using yarn A P20.
Rep last 2 rows 35 times more.
Cast off.

BORDER STRIPE SEQUENCE

Rows 1 to 10: Using yarn B.
Rows 11 to 22: Using yarn C.
Rows 23 to 33: Using yarn D.
Rows 34 to 36: Using yarn A.
Rows 37 to 62: Using yarn B.

Rows 63 to 72: Using yarns E and F held together.
Rows 73 to 82: Using yarns H and J held together.
Rows 83 to 86: Using yarn B.
Rows 87 to 101: Using yarn G.
Rows 102 to 110: Using yarn R.
Rows 111 to 141: Using yarns N and Q held together.
Rows 142 to 155: Using yarns L and M held together.
Rows 156 to 161: Using yarn A.
Rows 162 to 167: Using yarn R.
Rows 168 to 181: Using yarns H and J held together.
Rows 182 to 195: Using yarn D.
Rows 196 to 206: Using yarn C.
These 206 rows form border stripe sequence and are repeated as required.

END BORDERS (make 2)

Using 5mm (US 8) needles and yarn B, cast on 14 sts.
Beg with a K row, work in st st in border stripe sequence for 270 rows, ending with RS facing for next row. Cast off.

SIDE BORDERS (make 2)

Using 5mm (US 8) needles and yarn A, cast
on 14 sts.
Beg with a K row, work in st st for 20 rows,
ending with RS facing for next row.
Now work in border stripe sequence for 380
rows, ending with RS facing for next row.
Using yarn A, work a further 20 rows.
Cast off.

MAKING UP

Press as described on the information page.
Matching cast-on and cast-off edges of
panels, join left and right panels to sides of
centre panel using back stitch, or mattress
stitch if preferred. Sew end borders to cast-
on and cast-off edges, then sew side borders
to side edges of join sections.
Trim backing fabric to same size as joined
knitted sections, adding seam allowance
along all edges. Fold seam allowance to WS,
then slip stitch backing to WS of knitted
sections.

TEMPO BOLERO
Jean Moss

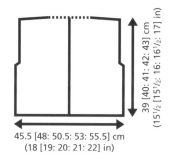

39 [40: 41: 42: 43] cm
(15½ [15½: 16: 16½: 17] in)

45.5 [48: 50.5: 53: 55.5] cm
(18 [19: 20: 21: 22] in)

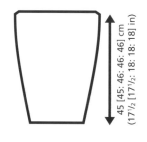

45 [45: 46: 46: 46] cm
(17½ [17½: 18: 18: 18] in)

SIZES & YARNS

XS	S	M	L	XL

To fit bust

81	86	91	97	102	cm
32	34	36	38	40	in

Rowan Scottish Tweed Aran

5	5	5	6	6	x 100gm

(photographed in Claret 013)

NEEDLES

1 pair 4mm (no 8) (US 6) needles
1 pair 5mm (no 6) (US 8) needles

TENSION

16 sts and 23 rows to 10 cm measured over
stocking stitch using 5mm (US 8) needles.

BACK

Using 4mm (US 6) needles, cast on 65 [69: 73: 77: 81] sts.

Row 1 (RS): K1, *P1, K1, rep from * to end.

Row 2: P1, *K1, P1, rep from * to end.

These 2 rows form rib.

Work in rib for a further 4 rows, ending with RS facing for next row.

Change to 5mm (US 8) needles.

Beg with a K row, work in st st, inc 1 st at each end of 3rd and every foll 10th row until there are 73 [77: 81: 85: 89] sts.

Cont straight until back meas 20 [21: 21: 22: 22] cm, ending with RS facing for next row.

Shape armholes

Dec 1 st at each end of next 5 rows. 63 [67: 71: 75: 79] sts.

Cont straight until armhole meas 19 [19: 20: 20: 21] cm, ending with RS facing for next row.

Shape shoulders

Cast off 9 [9: 10: 11: 12] sts at beg of next 2 rows, then 9 [10: 11: 11: 12] sts at beg of foll 2 rows.

Break yarn and leave rem 27 [29: 29: 31: 31] sts on a holder.

LEFT FRONT

Using 4mm (US 6) needles, cast on 38 [40: 42: 44: 46] sts.

Row 1 (RS): *K1, P1, rep from * to last 2 sts, K2.

Row 2: *K1, P1, rep from * to end.

These 2 rows form rib.

Work in rib for a further 4 rows, ending with RS facing for next row.

Change to 5mm (US 8) needles.

Row 7 (RS): K to last 7 sts, (P1, K1) 3 times, K1.

Row 8: K1, (P1, K1) 3 times, P to end.

These 2 rows set the sts.

Cont as set, inc 1 st at beg of next and every foll 10th row until there are 42 [44: 46: 48: 50] sts.

Cont straight until left front matches back to beg of armhole shaping, ending with RS facing for next row.

Shape armhole

Dec 1 st at beg of next row and at same edge on foll 4 rows. 37 [39: 41: 43: 45] sts.

Cont straight until left front matches back to beg of shoulder shaping, ending with RS facing for next row.

Shape shoulder

Cast off 9 [9: 10: 11: 12] sts at beg of next row, then 9 [10: 11: 11: 12] sts at beg of foll alt row.

Work 1 row, ending with RS facing for next row. Break yarn and leave rem 19 [20: 20: 21: 21] sts on a holder.

RIGHT FRONT

Using 4mm (US 6) needles, cast on 38 [40: 42: 44: 46] sts.

Row 1 (RS): K2, *P1, K1, rep from * to end.

Row 2: *P1, K1, rep from * to end.

These 2 rows form rib.

Work in rib for a further 4 rows, ending with RS facing for next row.

Change to 5mm (US 8) needles.

Row 7 (RS): K1, (K1, P1) 3 times, K to end.

Row 8: P to last 7 sts, (K1, P1) 3 times, K1.

These 2 rows set the sts.

Cont as set, inc 1 st at end of next and every foll 10th row until there are 42 [44: 46: 48: 50] sts.

Cont straight until right front matches back to beg of armhole shaping, ending with RS facing for next row.

Shape armhole

Dec 1 st at end of next row and at same edge on foll 4 rows. 37 [39: 41: 43: 45] sts.

Cont straight until right front matches back to beg of shoulder shaping, ending with WS facing for next row.

Shape shoulder

Cast off 9 [9: 10: 11: 12] sts at beg of next row, then 9 [10: 11: 11: 12] sts at beg of foll alt row, ending with RS facing for next row.

Do NOT break yarn (this ball of yarn will be used for collar) but leave rem 19 [20: 20: 21: 21] sts on a holder.

SLEEVES

Using 4mm (US 6) needles, cast on 41 [41: 43: 45: 45] sts.

Work in rib as given for back for 6 rows, ending with RS facing for next row.

Change to 5mm (US 8) needles.

Beg with a K row, work in st st, shaping sides by inc 1 st at each end of 5th [5th: 3rd: 5th: 3rd] and every foll 10th [10th: 8th: 10th: 8th] row to 57 [57: 49: 59: 61] sts, then on every foll 12th [12th: 10th: 12th: 10th] row until there are 59 [59: 63: 63: 67] sts.

Cont straight until sleeve meas 45 [45: 46: 46: 46] cm, ending with RS facing for next row.

Shape top

Dec 1 st at each end of next 5 rows, ending with WS facing for next row.

Cast off rem 49 [49: 53: 53: 57] sts purlwise (on WS).

MAKING UP

Press as described on the information page. Join both shoulder seams using back stitch, or mattress stitch if preferred.

Collar

With RS facing, using 5mm (US 8) needles and ball of yarn left with right front, patt 19 [20: 20: 21: 21] sts from right front holder, work across 27 [29: 29: 31: 31] back neck sts as folls: K0 [1: 1: 2: 2], (M1, K3) 9 times, M1, K0 [1: 1: 2: 2], then patt 19 [20: 20: 21: 21] sts from left front holder. 75 [79: 79: 83: 83] sts.

Keeping front opening edge sts correct as set and working all other sts in st st, cont as set until collar meas 13 cm from pick-up row, ending with RS facing for next row.

Working sts as set by front opening edge sts, work 4 rows in rib across all sts, ending with RS facing for next row.

Cast off in rib.

See information page for finishing instructions, setting in sleeves using the shallow set-in method.

FRILLY JACKET AND SKIRT
Sasha Kagan

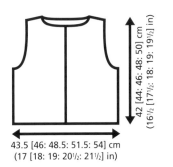

42 [44: 46: 48: 50] cm
(16½ [17½: 18: 19: 19½] in)

43.5 [46: 48.5: 51.5: 54] cm
(17 [18: 19: 20½: 21½] in)

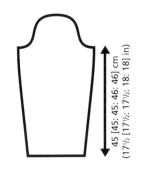

45 [45: 45: 46: 46] cm
(17½ [17½: 17½: 18: 18] in)

SIZES & YARNS

XS	S	M	L	XL	

To fit bust

| 81 | 86 | 91 | 97 | 102 | cm |
| 32 | 34 | 36 | 38 | 40 | in |

Rowan Scottish Tweed DK and 4ply

Jacket

A DK Storm Grey 004

| 8 | 9 | 9 | 10 | 11 | x 50gm |

B 4 ply Winter Navy 021

| 1 | 1 | 1 | 1 | 1 | x 25gm |

C 4 ply Skye 003

| 2 | 2 | 2 | 2 | 2 | x 25gm |

Skirt

A DK Celtic Mix 022

| 4 | 4 | 5 | 5 | 6 | x 50gm |

B 4 ply Mallard 020

| 2 | 2 | 2 | 2 | 2 | x 25gm |

C 4 ply Thistle 016

| 1 | 1 | 1 | 1 | 1 | x 25gm |

D 4 ply Claret 013

| 1 | 1 | 1 | 1 | 1 | x 25 gm |

HOOKS

1 4.00mm (no 8) (US G6) crochet hook
1 3.00mm (no 11) (US D3) crochet hook

TENSION

15 sts and 9 rows to 10 cm square measured over htr pattern using 4.00 mm (US G6) hook.

CROCHET ABBREVIATIONS

ch = chain; **ss** = slip stitch; **dc** = double crochet (= US single crochet); **htr** = half treble (= US half double); **yoh** = yarn over hook; **htr2tog** =*yoh and insert hook as indicated, yoh and draw through 2 loops; rep from * once more, yoh and draw through all 3 loops on hook (= US hdc2tog).

JACKET
BACK

With 4.00 mm (US G6) hook and A, make 66 [70: 74: 78: 82] ch.

Foundation row (RS): 1 htr into 3rd ch from hook, 1htr into each ch to end, turn 65 [69: 73: 77: 81] sts.

Row 1: 2 ch, miss first htr, working into front loop only, work 1 htr in each htr, 1 htr in top of 2 ch at beg of previous row, turn.

Row 2: 2 ch, miss first htr, working into back loop only, work 1 htr in each htr, 1 htr in top of 2 ch at beg of previous row, turn.

These 2 rows form the patt.

Cont in patt until Back meas 18 [19: 20: 21: 22]cm from beg, ending with RS facing for next row.

Shape armholes

Next row: Ss across first 5 [5: 6: 6: 7] sts, 2 ch, patt to last 4 [4: 5: 5: 6] sts, turn. 57 [61: 63: 67: 69] sts.

Dec row: 2 ch, miss first htr, work htr2tog, patt to last 3 sts, work htr2tog, 1 htr in top of 2 ch at beg of previous row, turn.

Rep the last row 4 [5: 5: 6: 6] times more. 47 [49: 51: 53: 55] sts.

Work straight until armhole meas 15 [16: 17: 18: 19]cm.

Shape back neck

Next row: 2 ch, miss first htr, patt 5 [5: 6: 6: 7] sts, work htr2tog, patt 1 st, turn.

Next row: 2 ch, miss first htr, work htr2tog, patt to end, turn.

Next row: 2 ch, miss first htr, patt 3 [3: 4: 4:

5] sts,work htr2tog, patt 1 st, turn.

Next row: 2 ch, miss first htr, work htr2tog, patt to end.

Fasten off.

5 [5: 6: 6: 7] sts.

Miss centre 29 [31: 31: 33: 33] sts, rejoin yarn to next st.

Next row: 2 ch, miss 1 htr, work htr2tog, patt to end, turn.

Next row: Patt to last 3 sts, work htr2tog, patt 1 st, turn.

Next row: 2 ch, miss first htr, work htr2tog, patt to end, turn.

Next row: Patt to last 3 sts, work htr2tog, patt 1 st, turn.

Fasten off.

5 [5: 6: 6: 7] sts.

POCKET LININGS (make 2)

With 4.00 mm (US G6) hook and A, make 15 [15: 17: 17: 19] ch.

Foundation row (RS): 1 htr into 3rd ch from hook, 1htr into each ch to end, turn. 14 [14: 16: 16: 18] sts.

Row 1: 2 ch, miss first htr, working into front loop only, work 1 htr in each htr, 1 htr in top of 2 ch at beg of previous row, turn.

Row 2: 2 ch, miss first htr, working into back loop only, work 1 htr in each htr, 1 htr in top of 2 ch at beg of previous row, turn.

Rep the last 2 rows twice and then row 1 again.

LEFT FRONT

With 4.00 mm (US G6) hook and A, make 27 [29:31:33:35] ch.

Foundation row (RS): 1 htr into 3rd ch from hook, 1htr into each ch to end, turn. 26 [28:30:32:34] sts.

Row 1: 2 ch, miss first htr, working into front loop only, work 1 htr in each htr, 1 htr in top of 2 ch at beg of previous row, turn.

Row 2: 2 ch, miss first htr, working into back loop only, work 1 htr in each htr, 1 htr in top of 2 ch at beg of previous row, turn.

These 2 rows form the patt.

Rep the last 2 rows twice more and row 1 again, ending with RS facing for next row.

Place pocket

Next row: 2 ch, miss first htr, working into back loop only, work 1 htr in each of next 8 [9:9:10:10] htr, 1 htr in each of 14

[14:16:16:18] sts across pocket, miss 14 [14:16:16:18] sts on front, 1 htr in each of next 2 [3:3:4:4] htr, 1 htr in top of 2 ch at beg of previous row, turn.

Cont in patt, until Left Front meas 18 [19: 20: 21: 22] cm from beg ending with a RS facing for next row.

Shape armhole

Next row: Ss across next 5 [5: 6: 6: 7] sts, 2 ch, patt to end, turn. 22 [24: 25: 27: 28] sts.
Working decreases as for back, dec 1 st at armhole edge on next 5 [6: 6: 7: 7] rows.
17 [18: 19: 20: 21] sts.
Work 2 [3: 3: 4: 4] rows, ending with a RS facing of next row.

Shape neck

Next row: Patt to last 7 [8: 8: 9: 9] sts, turn.
Dec 1 st at neck edge on every row until 5 [5:6:6:7] sts rem.
Work straight until Left Front matches same as Back to shoulder.
Fasten off.

RIGHT FRONT

Work to match Left Front, reversing all shapings and pocket position.

SLEEVES

With 4.00 mm (US G6) hook and A, make 27 [29: 31: 33: 35] ch.

Foundation row (RS): 1 htr into 3rd ch from hook, 1htr into each ch to end, turn. 26 [28: 30: 32: 34] sts.

Row 1: 2 ch, miss first htr, working into front loop only, work 1 htr in each htr, 1 htr in top of 2 ch at beg of previous row, turn.

Row 2: 2 ch, miss first htr, working into back loop only, work 1 htr in each htr, 1 htr in top of 2 ch at beg of previous row, turn.
These 2 rows form the patt.

Next row: 2 ch, miss first htr, working into front loop only, work 1 htr in each of next 5 htr, 2 htr into next htr, 1 htr into each htr to last 6 htr, 2 htr into next htr, 1 htr in each of next 5 htr, 1 tr into top of 2 ch at beg of previous row, turn.
28 [30: 32: 34: 36] sts.
Working all increases as set by last row, cont in treble patt, inc 1 st at each end of every foll 4th row until there are 42 [44: 46: 48: 50] sts.
Cont straight until Sleeve meas 40 [40: 40: 41: 41] cm.

Shape top

Next row: Ss across next 5[5:6:6:7] sts, 2 ch, patt to last 4 [4: 5: 5: 6] sts, turn.
34 [36: 36: 38: 38] sts.

Dec row: 2 ch, miss first htr, work htr2tog, patt to last 3 sts, work htr2tog, 1 htr in top of 2 ch at beg of previous row, turn.
Patt 1 row.
Rep the last 2 rows 2 [3:3:4:4] times more.
28 sts.
Dec 1 st at each end of the next 3 rows.
22 sts.
Fasten off.

EDGING

Join side and shoulder seams.
With RS facing, using 4.00mm (US G6) hook join A to right side seam.

Foundation round: 1 dc in each ch to corner, 3 dc into corner, work in dc up right front to shoulder, round back neck and down left front to corner, 3 dc into corner, 1 dc in each ch to beg of round, ss in first dc, turn.
To keep fabric flat, work 3 htr in each corner and dec 4 htr round back on each of the next 4 rows.

Round 1: 2 ch, miss first st, working into front loop only, work 1 htr in each st, ss in top of 2 ch at beg of round, turn.

Round 2: 2 ch, miss first htr, working into back loop only, work 1 htr in each htr, 1 htr in top of 2 ch at beg of round, turn.
Rep the last 2 rows once more.
Fasten off.
With RS facing, 3.00mm (US D3) crochet hook join B to beg of round, work one ss in each st, join with a ss.
Fasten off.
With RS facing, 3.00mm (US D/3) crochet hook join C to first missed loop of foundation round, work one ss in each missed loop, join with a ss.
Fasten off,

Frill
With RS facing, 3.00mm (US D/3) crochet hook join C to beg of first missed loop of round 2.

Round 1: Work 1 dc in each missed loop to end, join with a ss, turn.

Round 2: Work 2 dc in each dc, join with a ss, turn.

Round 3 * (1dc, 1ch) twice in next dc; rep

from * to end of round, join with a ss.
Fasten off.

LOWER SLEEVE EDGING

With RS facing, using 4.00mm (US G6) hook join M to first ch of lower edge of Sleeve.

Foundation row: 1 dc in each ch to end, turn.

Row 1: 2 ch, miss first st, working into front loop only, work 1 htr in each st, turn.

Row 2: 2 ch, miss first htr, working into back loop only, work 1 htr in each htr, 1 htr in top of 2 ch at beg of row, turn.

Rep the last 2 rows once more.

Fasten off.

With RS facing, 3.00mm (US D3) crochet hook join B to beg of row, work 1 ss in each st to end.

Fasten off.

With RS facing, 3.00mm (US D3) crochet hook join C to first missed loop of foundation row, work 1 ss in each missed loop to end.

Fasten off.

Frill

With RS facing, 3.00mm (US D3) crochet hook join C to beg of first missed loop of row 2.

Row 1: Work 1 dc in each missed loop to end, turn.

Row 2: Work 2 dc in each dc, turn.

Row 3: * (1dc, 1ch) twice in next dc; rep from * to end of row.

Fasten off.

MAKING UP

Press as described on the information page.
Join sleeve seams. Insert Sleeves.
Sew pocket linings in place to WS.

SKIRT

BACK AND FRONT (both alike)

With 4.00 mm (US G6) hook and M, make 66 [70:74:78:82] ch.

Foundation row (RS): 1 htr into 3rd ch from hook, 1htr into each ch to end, turn. 65 [69:73:77:81] sts.

Row 1: 2 ch, miss first htr, working into front loop only, work 1 htr in each htr, 1 htr in top of 2 ch at beg of previous row, turn.

Row 2: 2 ch, miss first htr, working into back loop only, work 1 htr in each htr, 1 htr in top of 2 ch at beg of previous row, turn.

These 2 rows form the patt.

Cont in patt until work meas 22 [23: 24: 25: 26] cm from beg ending with a RS facing for next row.

Dec row: 2 ch, miss 1 htr, 1 htr in each of next 8 htr, work htr2tog, patt to last 11 sts, work htr2tog, 1 htr in each of next 8 htr, 1 htr in top of 2 ch at beg of previous row, turn.

Patt 1 row.

Rep the last 2 rows 7 times more.
49 [53:57:61:65] sts.

Eyelet row: 3 ch, miss first 2 htr, * 1 htr in next htr, 1ch; rep from to end, 1htr in top of 2 ch, turn.

Next row: 2 ch, * 1htr in next ch, 1 htr in next htr, rep from * to end, 1htr in next ch, 1htr in top of 2 ch.

Fasten off.

Single stripes

Worked along the 4th, 8th and 12 rows of missed loops.

With RS facing, 3.00mm (US D3) crochet hook join B to beg of row, work one ss in each st to end.

Fasten off.

Frills

Worked along the 2nd (worked in C), 6th (worked in D) and 10th (worked in C) rows of missed loops.

With RS facing, 3.00mm (US D3) crochet hook join appropriate yarn to beg of first missed loop of row.

Row 1: Work 1 dc in each missed loop to end, turn.

Row 2: Work 2 dc in each dc, turn.

Row 3: * (1dc, 1ch) twice in next dc; rep from * to end of row.

Fasten off.

MAKING UP

Press as described on the information page.
Join side seams.
Using 4 strands of C make a twisted cord 200 cm long. Thread through eyelets to tie at centre front.
Using B and D make two pon-poms, each 5 cm in diameter. Attach one to each end of twisted cord.

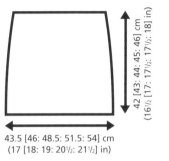

42 [43: 44: 45: 46] cm
(16½ [17: 17½: 17½: 18] in)

43.5 [46: 48.5: 51.5: 54] cm
(17 [18: 19: 20½: 21½] in)

USEFUL INFORMATION

TENSION

Obtaining the correct tension is perhaps the single factor which can make the difference between a successful garment and a disastrous one. It controls both the shape and size of an article, so any variation, however slight, can distort the finished garment. Different designers feature in our books and it is their tension, given at the start of each pattern, which you must match. We recommend that you knit a square in pattern and/or stocking stitch (depending on the pattern instructions) of perhaps 5-10 more stitches and 5-10 more rows than those given in the tension note. Mark out the central 10cm square with pins. If you have too many stitches to 10cm try again using thicker needles, if you have too few stitches to 10cm try again using finer needles. Once you have achieved the correct tension your garment will be knitted to the measurements indicated in the size diagram shown at the end of the pattern.

SIZING & SIZE DIAGRAM NOTE

The instructions are given for the smallest size. Where they vary, work the figures in brackets for the larger sizes. One set of figures refers to all sizes. Included with most patterns in this magazine is a "size diagram", or sketch of the finished garment and its dimensions. The size diagram shows the finished width of the garment at the under-arm point, and it is this measurement that the knitter should choose first; a useful tip is to measure one of your own garments which is a comfortable fit. Having chosen a size based on width, look at the corresponding length for that size; if you are not happy with the total length which we recommend, adjust your own garment before beginning your armhole shaping – any adjustment after this point will mean that your sleeve will not fit into your garment easily. Don't forget to take your adjustment into account if there is any side seam shaping. Finally, look at the sleeve length; the size diagram shows the finished sleeve measurement, taking into account any top-arm insertion length. Measure your body between the centre of your neck and your wrist, this measurement should correspond to half the garment width

plus the sleeve length. Again, your sleeve length may be adjusted, but remember to take into consideration your sleeve increases if you do adjust the length – you must increase more frequently than the pattern states to shorten your sleeve, less frequently to lengthen it.

CHART NOTE

Many of the patterns in the book are worked from charts. Each square on a chart represents a stitch and each line of squares a row of knitting. Each colour used is given a different letter and these are shown in the materials section, or in the key alongside the chart of each pattern. When working from the charts, read odd rows (K) from right to left and even rows (P) from left to right, unless otherwise stated.

KNITTING WITH COLOUR

There are two main methods of working colour into a knitted fabric: Intarsia and Fair Isle techniques. The first method produces a single thickness of fabric and is usually used where a colour is only required in a particular area of a row and does not form a repeating pattern across the row, as in the Fair Isle technique.

Intarsia: The simplest way to do this is to cut short lengths of yarn for each motif or block of colour used in a row. Then joining in the various colours at the appropriate point on the row, link one colour to the next by twisting them around each other where they meet on the wrong side to avoid gaps. All ends can then either be darned along the colour join lines, as each motif is completed or then can be "knitted-in" to the fabric of the knitting as each colour is worked into the pattern. This is done in much the same way as "weaving-in" yarns when working the Fair Isle technique and does save time darning-in ends. It is essential that the tension is noted for Intarsia as this may vary from the stocking stitch if both are used in the same pattern.

Fair isle type knitting: When two or three colours are worked repeatedly across a row, strand the yarn not in use loosely behind the stitches being worked. If you are working with more than two colours, treat the "floating" yarns as if they were one yarn and always spread the stitches to their correct width to keep them elastic. It is advisable not to carry the stranded or "floating" yarns over more than three stitches at a time, but to weave them under and over the colour you are working. The "floating" yarns are therefore caught at the back of the work.

SLIP STITCH EDGINGS

When a row end edge forms the actual finished edge of a garment, you will often find a slip stitch edging is worked along this edge. To work a slip stitch edging at the end of a RS row, work across the row until there is one stitch left on the left needle. Pick up the loop lying between the needles and place this loop on the right needle. Please note that this loop does NOT count as a stitch and is not included in any stitch counts. Now slip the last stitch knitwise with the yarn at the back (WS) of the work. At the beginning of the next row P together the first (slipped) stitch with the picked-up loop. To work a slip stitch edging at the end of a WS row, work across the row until there is one stitch left on the left needle. Pick up the loop lying

between the needles and place this loop on the right needle. Please note that this loop does NOT count as a stitch and is not included in any stitch counts. Now slip the last stitch purlwise with the yarn at the front (WS) of the work. At the beginning of the next row K together tbl the first (slipped) stitch with the picked-up loop.

FINISHING INSTRUCTIONS

After working for hours knitting a garment, it seems a great pity that many garments are spoiled because such little care is taken in the pressing and finishing process. Follow the following tips for a truly professional-looking garment.

PRESSING

Block out each piece of knitting and following the instructions on the ball band press the garment pieces, omitting the ribs.
Tip: Take special care to press the edges, as this will make sewing up both easier and neater.
If the ball band indicates that the fabric is not to be pressed, then covering the blocked

out fabric with a damp white cotton cloth and leaving it to stand will have the desired effect. Darn in all ends neatly along the selvage edge or a colour join, as appropriate.

STITCHING

When stitching the pieces together, remember to match areas of colour and texture very carefully where they meet. Use a seam stitch such as back stitch or mattress stitch for all main knitting seams and join all ribs and neckband with mattress stitch, unless otherwise stated.

CONSTRUCTION

Having completed the pattern instructions, join left shoulder and neckband seams as detailed above. Sew the top of the sleeve to the body of the garment using the method detailed in the pattern, referring to the appropriate guide:
Straight cast-off sleeves: Place centre of cast-off edge of sleeve to shoulder seam. Sew top of sleeve to body, using markers as guidelines where applicable.
Square set-in sleeves: Place centre of cast-

off edge of sleeve to shoulder seam. Set sleeve head into armhole, the straight sides at top of sleeve to form a neat right-angle to cast-off sts at armhole on back and front.
Shallow set-in sleeves: Place centre of cast off edge of sleeve to shoulder seam. Match decreases at beg of armhole shaping to decreases at top of sleeve. Sew sleeve head into armhole, easing in shapings.
Set-in sleeves: Place centre of cast-off edge of sleeve to shoulder seam. Set in sleeve, easing sleeve head into armhole. Join side and sleeve seams. Slip stitch pocket edgings and linings into place. Sew on buttons to correspond with buttonholes. Ribbed welts and neckbands and any areas of garter stitch should not be pressed.

ABBREVIATIONS

YARN INFORMATION

1	7	13	19
2	8	14	20
3	9	15	21
4	10	16	22
5	11	17	23
6	12	18	24

K	knit
P	purl
st(s)	stitch(es)
inc	increas(e)(ing)
dec	decreas(e)(ing)
st st	stocking stitch (K all RS rows, P all WS rows)
g st	garter stitch (K every row)
beg	begin(ning)
foll	following
rem	remain(ing)
rev st st	reverse stocking stitch (P all RS rows, K all WS rows)
rep	repeat
alt	alternate
cont	continue
patt	pattern
tog	together
mm	millimetres
cm	centimetres
in	inch(es)
RS	right side
WS	wrong side
sl 1	slip one stitch
psso	pass slipped stitch over
p2sso	pass 2 slipped stitches over

tbl	through back of loop
M1	make one stitch by picking up horizontal loop before next stitch and knitting into back of it
M1P	make one stitch by picking up horizontal loop before next stitch and purling into back of it
yfwd	yarn forward (= US yo – yarn over)
yrn	yarn round needle (= US yo – yarn over)
meas	measures
0	no stitches, times or rows – no stitches, times or rows for that size

Note: See pattern instructions (eg page 92) for crochet abbreviations.

Rowan Scottish Tweed Yarns (formerly known as Harris Yarns) are available in four weights: 4 ply, DK, Aran and Chunky. The full range of colours available in 4 ply is shown right. The other weights come in some but not all of these colours. All the yarns are to be hand washed or can be dry cleaned at the cleaner's discretion.

Rowan Scottish Tweed 4 ply
A lightweight 100 per cent pure new wool yarn
Ball size: 25g (1oz); about 110m (120yds) per ball
Recommended tension: 26-28 sts and 38-40 rows to 10cm (4in) using needle size 3-3¼mm/11-10 UK (2-3 US)

Rowan Scottish Tweed DK
A medium-weight 100 per cent pure new wool yarn
Ball size: 50g (1¾oz); about 113m (123yds) per ball.
Recommended tension: 20-22 sts and 28-30 rows to 10cm (4in) using needle size 4mm/8 UK (6 US)

Rowan Scottish Tweed Aran
A thick 100 per cent pure new wool yarn
Ball size: 100g (3½oz); about 170m (186yds) per ball
Recommended tension: 16 sts and 23 rows to 10cm (4in) using needle size 5-5½mm/6-5 UK (8-9 US)

Rowan Scottish Tweed Chunky
A chunky 100 per cent pure new wool yarn
Ball size: 100g (3½oz); about 100m (109yds) per ball.
Recommended tension: 12 sts and 16 rows to 10cm (4in) using needle size 8mm/0 UK (11 US)

1. Lobster 017
2. Rust 009
3. Brilliant pink 010
4. Sunset 011
5. Wine 012
6. Claret 013
7. Apple 015
8. Thatch 018
9. Celtic mix 022
10. Herring 008
11. Heath 014
12. Peat 019
13. Skye 003
14. Machair 002
15. Sea green 006
16. Mallard 020
17. Winter navy 021
18. Midnight 023
19. Thistle 016
20. Lavender 005
21. Porridge 024
22. Grey mist 001
23. Storm grey 004
24. Lewis grey 007

AUSTRALIA
Australian Country Spinners,
314 Albert Street,
Brunswick, Victoria 3056.
Tel: (03) 9380 3888

BELGIUM
Pavan, Meerlaanstraat 73,
B9860 Balegem (Oosterzele).
Tel: (32) 9 221 8594
pavan@pandora.be

CANADA
Diamond Yarn, 9697 St
Laurent, Montreal, Quebec,
H3L 2N1.
Tel: (514) 388 6188
Diamond Yarn (Toronto),
155 Martin Ross, Unit 3,
Toronto, Ontario, M3J 2L9.
Tel: (416) 736 6111
diamond@diamondyarn.com
www.diamondyarns.com

DENMARK
AALBORG:
Designvaerkstedet,
Boulevarden 9, 9000.
Tel: (45) 9812 0713
Fax: (45) 9813 0213
AARHUS: Ingerís, Volden 19,
8000. Tel: (45) 8619 4044

KOBENHAVN K:
Sommerfuglen, Vandkunsten
3, 1467. Tel: (45) 3332 8290
mail@sommerfuglen.dk
www.sommerfuglen.dk
KOBENHAVN K: Uldstedet,
Fiolstraede 13, 1171.
Tel/Fax: (45) 3391 1771
LYNGBY: Uldstedet, G1,
Jernbanevej 7, 2800.
Tel/Fax: (45) 4588 1088
ROSKILDE: Garnhoekeren,
Karen Olsdatterstraede 9,
4000.
Tel/Fax: (45) 4637 2063

FRANCE
Elle Tricot: 8 Rue du Coq,
67000 Strasbourg.
Tel: (33) 3 88 23 03 13
HYPERLINK
"mailto:elletricot@agat.net"
elletricot@agat.net
www.elletricote.com

GERMANY
Wolle & Design,
Wolfshovener Strasse 76,
52428 Julich-Stetternich.
Tel: (49) 2461 54735.
Info@wolleunddesign.de
www.wolleunddesign.de

HOLLAND
de Afstap, Oude Leliestraat
12, 1015 AW Amsterdam.
Tel: (31) 20 6231445

HONG KONG
East Unity Co Ltd, Unit B2,
7/F Block B, Kailey Industrial
Centre, 12 Fung Yip Street,
Chai Wan.
Tel: (852) 2869 7110
Fax (852) 2537 6952
eastuni@netvigator.com

ICELAND
Storkurinn, Laugavegi 59,
101 Reykjavik.
Tel: (354) 551 8258
Fax: (354) 562 8252
malin@mmedia.is

JAPAN
Puppy Co Ltd, T151-0051,
3-16-5 Sendagaya,
Shibuyaku, Tokyo.
Tel: (81) 3 3490 2827
info@rowan-jaeger.com

KOREA
De Win Co Ltd, Chongam
Bldg, 101, 34-7 Samsung-
dong, Seoul.

Tel: (82) 2 511 1087.
knittking@yahoo.co.kr.
Www.dewin.co.kr
My Knit Studio, (3F) 121
Kwan Hoon Dong, Chongro
- ku, Seoul,
Tel: (82) 2 722 0006.
myknit@myknit.com

NEW ZEALAND
AUCKLAND: Alterknitives,
PO Box 47961, Ponsonby.
Tel: (64) 9 376 0337
knitit@ihug.co.nz
LOWER HUTT: Knit World,
PO Box 30 645.
Tel: (64) 4 586 4530
knitting@xtra.co.nz
TAUPO: The Stitchery,
Shop 8, Suncourt Shopping
Centre, 1111 Taupo.
Tel: (64) 7 378

NORWAY
Paa Pinne, Tennisvn 3D,
0777 Oslo.
Tel: (47) 909 62 818
design@paapinne.no
www.paapinne.no

SPAIN
Oyambre, Pau Claris 145,

80009 Barcelona.
Tel: (34) 670 011957
comercial@oyambreonline.
com

SWEDEN
Wincent, Norrtullsgatan 65,
113 45 Stockholm.
Tel: (46) 8 33 70 60
wincent@chello.se
www.wincent.nu

U.S.A.
Rowan USA, c/o
Westminster Fibers Inc, 4
Townsend West, Suite 8,
Nashua, NH 03063
Tel: (1 603) 886 5041/5043.
rowan@westminsterfibers.
com

For All Other Countries:
please contact Rowan for
stockists details.

The publishers would like to thank the
designers – Kaffe Fassett, Di Gilpin,
Sarah Dallas, Jean Moss, Sasha Kagan,
Brandon Mably and Sarah Hatton – and the
pattern writers, pattern checkers and knitters
for their work on this book, in particular
Sue Whiting, Stella Smith and Penny Hill.

They would also like to thank Jacqui Hurst
for her photography, as well as Peter
Williams for his initial help, Georgina Rhodes
and Richard Proctor for the design, art
direction and styling, Chloe Palmer,
Bluebell Martin and Oskar Proctor for
modelling, Sally Harding for editorial help,
and Steve McKay of Harris Tweed Textiles
for his help.